*George S. Counts
and American Civilization*

George S. Counts
and American Civilization
The Educator
as Social Theorist

by
GERALD L. GUTEK

MERCER

All books published by Mercer University are produced on acid-free paper that exceeds
the minimum standards set by the National Historical Publications and
Records Commission.

Library of Congress Cataloging in Publication Data

Gutek, Gerald Lee.
   George S. Counts and American civilization.

   Bibliography: p. 163.
   Includes index.
   1. Counts, George S. (George Sylvester), 1889-1974.   2. Social scientists—United
States—Biography.   3. United States—Civilization.   4. United States—Social
conditions.
   I. Title.
H59.C68G87   1984   300'.92'4 [B]   83-23762
ISBN 0-86554-091-8 (alk. paper)

Contents

Preface 1

Chapter 1
George S. Counts:
The Man and the Scholar 3

Chapter 2
The Depression of the 1930s:
An Educator Reacts to Crisis 15

Chapter 3
Counts's Frame of Reference 29

Chapter 4
Crisis Between Two Civilizations 43

Chapter 5
The Democratic Heritage in a Technological Age 61

Chapter 6
Economic Individualism and the American Experience 77

Chapter 7
Counts's Program of Action 97

Chapter 8
Counts's Civilizational Philosophy of Education 123

Chapter 9
  The Impact of Counts's Analysis of Soviet Education
  on His Theory of American Civilization........................... 137
Chapter 10
  George S. Counts and American Political Reform.................149
Bibliography 163
Index..169

Preface

The chapters that follow are intended to examine the interpretation of American civilization that was developed by George S. Counts, one of the leading educational theorists of the United States. During his long career, Counts distinguished himself as a professor of educational history, sociologist of education, educational philosopher, and comparative educator. He won the respect of his colleagues for his research and writing on American and Soviet education. At various stages in his career, he was a leading voice in progressive educational circles, a president of the American Federation of Teachers, and a candidate for political office.

This focus looks at Counts as a social theorist who developed a conception of American civilization; it will not be concerned with Counts's views of school organization, curriculum, or instructional methodology. Although he made important contributions to these areas of American professional education, the aim of this book is to examine Counts as a social theorist who saw education in broad cultural terms.

In part, this study centers on Counts as a theorist during the decade of America's Great Depression, the 1930s. It was this period that seemed to sharpen his insights into American civilization and its prospects. While the Depression period was a crucial decade in Counts's career, it was but one segment of his productive life. I hope that my treatment of Counts, with its particular focus, will illuminate the process by which a leading educator entered into the arena of social and political analysis.

I wish to express my appreciation to the research committee of Loyola University of Chicago for a grant that aided in the publication of this book. I also want to thank Miss Marla Gee, who typed the manuscript with great patience and care.

Gerald L. Gutek
Loyola University of Chicago

Chapter 1

George S. Counts: The Man and the Scholar

With the death of George S. Counts on 10 November 1974, American education lost a statesman who had made the study of American civilization a lifelong career. Well known as an educational theorist, Counts was also a social theorist who had carefully scrutinized the origins, development, and problems of American civilization. Counts's contributions to American education have been described in textbooks and analyzed in specialized studies.[1] However, Counts's conception of American civilization has not received the analysis that it deserves. In examining the theory of American civilization that was developed by George Sylvester Counts, this book will highlight his response to the Depression of the 1930s.

Counts, who believed that the people of the United States had developed a uniquely democratic and particularly American concept of civilization, was also convinced that the industrial revolution had profoundly changed life on this planet. In particular, a technological social order had emerged that had the potentiality of both eroding and nourishing the American democratic heritage. He regarded it as his personal, civic, and academic responsibility to examine American civilization in its technological era. In pursuing his charge, Counts developed a

---

[1]Counts's educational theory is examined in Gerald L. Gutek, *The Educational Theory of George S. Counts* (Columbus: Ohio State University Press, 1970).

theory of American civilization and social change that was a broad synthesis drawn from the work of American economists, historians, political scientists, and educators.

Textbooks in the history of American education give Counts prominence as the author of *Dare the School Build a New Social Order?* This profound but also polemical question was raised during the crisis of the Great Depression of the 1930s.[2] Counts argued that all life, indeed all education, is based on a particular civilization at a particular time in history. It is within his own context of cultural relativism that certain aspects of Counts's social theory can be interpreted within the climate of the Depression era.

Counts believed that his basic thesis held a meaning for American life that transcended the decade of Roosevelt and the New Deal.[3] Although the Depression era served as a catalyst that stimulated Counts to articulate his theory of American civilization, his interpretation of American culture and social change has had a more enduring meaning. What Counts really developed was a theory that explained the modernization of American life and identified both the dangers and the potentialities inherent in that process. The pages that follow examine Counts's social theory in the context of the Depression milieu and also treat the concepts that have relevance for today. In initiating this analysis, it is appropriate to begin with the man himself.

George S. Counts:
Educational Statesman

In a biographical sketch in *Leaders in American Education*, Raymond E. Callahan called George S. Counts an "Educational Statesman." A former student of Counts, Callahan referred to his mentor as the "Walter Lippman of education." Like

---

[2]The context of Counts's *Dare the School Build a New Social Order?* is examined in C. A. Bowers, *The Progressive Educator and the Depression: The Radical Years* (New York: Random House, 1969) 3-47.

[3]Interview with George S. Counts by the author in December 1963.

Lippmann, Counts possessed "a gifted pen," "penetrating insight," and the "ability to get to the heart of a matter." In commenting on Counts as an educational statesman, Callahan found him to be "a kind of conscience for American educators," who in his analysis of American society and education sought to "humanize human society" and to "make the world a place where men could live decently and with dignity."[4]

George Sylvester Counts, the son of James and Mertie Gamble Counts, was born on 9 December 1889, on the family farm located near Baldwin, Kansas. In reminiscing about his childhood, Counts recalled that "in the old agrarian society there was a place for the child." It was "the farm household and the farm neighborhood that provided most of the education for the youngster." He stated:

> I can remember when I was allowed to drive a team of horses with a plow. I was about 13. I stayed out of school when I was 13 because my parents thought I wasn't old enough to go on to high school or to continue in high school, so I stayed out a whole year. I remember what I did that year. In the spring I took a team of horses and I had my first experience with a plow, in the field. And so it went. The individual boy or girl had his or her responsibilities, his work to do in the household and in various other places around the farm.[5]

Counts's first two years of formal education were in a one-room country school that housed all eight grades. When the family moved to another farm nearer to town, he attended Baldwin's public elementary and high schools, from which he graduated in 1907.

Attending Baker University, a Methodist institution located in Baldwin, Counts majored as an undergraduate in the classical

---

[4]Raymond E. Callahan, "George S. Counts: Educational Statesman," in Robert J. Havighurst, ed., *Leaders in American Education: The Seventieth Yearbook of the National Society for the Study of Education* (Chicago: University of Chicago Press, 1971) 177, 179.

[5]"Interview with Dr. George Counts—Southern Illinois University—21 September 1964," in Special Collections/Morris Library, Southern Illinois University at Carbondale. (Interview was conducted by Mr. Seyfert.)

studies of Greek and Latin. He also enrolled in courses in the natural sciences, history, and philosophy. His autobiographical account mentioned several of his professors: Homer K. Enright in Greek, O. G. Markham in Latin, Joseph K. Hart in philosophy, Charles S. Parmenter in biology, and Alice D. Porter in English literature.[6] While a student at Baker University, Counts was active in student activities and athletics. He was a member of the varsity basketball and football teams. In 1911 Baker University awarded him the degree of bachelor of arts in classical studies.

Although he had not prepared specifically for a teaching career while a student at Baker University, upon graduation Counts decided in 1911 to take a position as a mathematics and science teacher in the Sumner County High School in Wellington, Kansas. He then took a position, for the school year 1912-1913, as principal of the high school in Peabody, Kansas, where he taught mathematics and science and coached athletics in addition to performing his administrative duties. On 24 September 1913, Counts married Lois Hazel Bailey.

For graduate study, Counts was attracted to the University of Chicago, which he regarded as "a champion of radical ideas in the fields of biology, social science, philosophy, and theology."[7] Beginning his graduate study in 1913 at Chicago, he studied with a number of respected educators and social scientists who were establishing the standards of excellence in their disciplines. His adviser was Charles Hubbard Judd, dean of the School of Education and a distinguished psychologist. In commenting on Judd, Counts recalled that although his mentor was "a very distinguished man," he did not agree "with some of the positions he took."[8] Counts was the first of Judd's students to select a minor in sociology and the social sciences, rather than in psychology. He also worked with Franklin Bobbitt, a pioneer in the

[6]George S. Counts, "A Humble Autobiography," in Havighurst, *Leaders in American Education*, 151-74.

[7]Ibid., 158.

[8]"Interview with Counts," Special Collections.

area of the school curriculum. In addition to his program in professional education, Counts was attracted to the social science field, and took courses with Albion W. Small, head of the Department of Sociology, and William I. Thomas, a leader in American social theory. Among his other professors were Frederick Starr in anthropology, Charles E. Merriam in political science, and Harold G. Moulton in economics. In 1916 the University of Chicago awarded Counts the degree of doctor of philosophy with specialization in education and the social sciences.

In addition to his teachers and professors, Counts acknowledged the influence of his fellow scholars and associates in politics and union activities. Personally acquainted with John Dewey, the famous proponent of instrumentalist philosophy, he worked with Dewey on the committees of the Liberal party in New York State. Counts generally shared an allegiance to Dewey's pragmatic orientation in philosophy, politics, and education. Counts also worked with his close friend Charles A. Beard on the Commission of the American Historical Association on the Social Studies in the Schools. Counts's view of the American democratic heritage was influenced by Beard's economic interpretation of history.

In 1916 Counts joined the staff of Delaware College as head of the Department of Education and director of the summer school. In 1918 he taught at Harris Teachers College in St. Louis; in 1919 at the University of Washington; in 1920 at Yale University; in 1926 at the University of Chicago.

From 1927 until his retirement in 1955, Counts taught at Teachers College, Columbia University, where he was a member of an eminent group of educators who developed the major social and philosophical orientations that shaped American education in the first half of the twentieth century. In helping to build the foundations of education at Teachers College, Counts was a colleague of Jesse Newlon, John L. Childs, William Heard Kilpatrick, William F. Russell, Harold Rugg, and F. Ernest Johnson. It was during his Teachers College years that he developed his theory of American civilization. After retiring from Teachers College, Counts was a much-sought-after visiting professor. He taught at the University of Pittsburgh, the University of Colorado, Michigan State University, Northwestern University, and Southern Illinois University.

Beyond his study of American culture and education, Counts also was a recognized scholar in comparative education, especially in Soviet education. His actual work in comparative education began in 1925 when he was a member of the Educational Survey Commission to the Philippines. When he joined the faculty of Columbia University Teachers College in 1927, he was appointed associate director of the International Institute.

In comparative education, Counts's major concentration was the study of Soviet society and education. Counts's first trip to the Soviet Union in 1927 enabled him to study the Russian language and to examine Soviet social, economic, political, and educational institutions, policies, and practices. In 1929 Counts undertook a memorable visit to the Soviet Union, then in the midst of its First Five Year Plan. His travel diary records his impressions as he drove a Model A Ford automobile on a 6,000-mile journey through the Soviet Union.[9] Counts, who published an account of his travels in the Soviet Union in *A Ford Crosses Soviet Russia*, 1930, observed that "the traveler, however, does not see the new social order appearing merely in material construction and the reorganization of institutions." If he were to direct his attention to the people, "he would know that a new society is in the making."[10]

The following year, 1931, saw the publication of Counts's first comprehensive treatment of Soviet culture and education, *The Soviet Challenge to America*, which contained detailed analysis of the implementation of the First Five Year Plan.[11] Counts's commentaries on Soviet society and education written in the 1930s reveal an interest in Soviet planning, social reorganiza-

---

[9]George S. Counts, "Diary of Auto Tour in Soviet Union," George S. Counts Papers, Special Collections/Morris Library, Southern Illinois University at Carbondale.

[10]George S. Counts, *A Ford Crosses Soviet Russia* (Boston: The Stratford Co., 1930) 170.

[11]George S. Counts, *The Soviet Challenge to America* (New York: John Day Co., 1931).

tion, and modernization. They also show that Counts's impressions of the Soviet system did not penetrate to a realization of its underlying totalitarian nature. In 1936 Counts made his last trip to the Soviet Union. By the 1940s Counts, now a critic of the Soviet system, was no longer permitted to enter the Soviet Union. With Nucia P. Lodge, he wrote *The Country of the Blind: the Soviet System of Mind Control.*[12] In 1957 Counts's *The Challenge of Soviet Education* appeared. As a mature and scholarly examination of Soviet culture and education, *The Challenge of Soviet Education* analyzed the ideological foundations of the Soviet system.[13] This book received the Liberty and Justice Award of the American Library Association, which called it "the most distinguished book of 1957 in contemporary problems and affairs."

Supplementing his work on Soviet culture and education, Counts developed an international perspective on education. During his career, he visited seventeen countries to study their social and educational systems; he lectured in eleven of those countries. In 1948 he was a member of the educational mission that advised General Douglas MacArthur on the democratic reconstruction of Japanese education.

Concerned with formulating educational policies and implementing social and educational theories, Counts was a member of national committees of the Progressive Education Association, the National Education Association, and the American Historical Association. He was the research director of the Commission of the American Historical Association on the Social Studies in the Schools. From 1936 to 1942, he was a member of the Educational Policies Commission of the National Educational Association. Counts's participation in these national committees helped to imprint his thought on American democracy in a time of profound social and economic transition.

---

[12]George S. Counts and Nucia P. Lodge, *The Country of the Blind: The Soviet System of Mind Control* (Boston: Houghton Mifflin Co., 1949).

[13]George S. Counts, *The Challenge of Soviet Education* (New York: McGraw-Hill Book Co., 1957).

Counts, who consistently supported trade and industrial union movements, advocated teacher unionization. From 1939 to 1941, he was president of the American Federation of Teachers. One of the major issues in his election in 1939 and reelection in 1940 was his effort to eliminate Communist influence from the American Federation of Teachers. In bitterly contested elections, his victories helped to free the American Federation of Teachers from Communist influence. While Counts opposed Communist machinations to control the teachers union, he also opposed the "red baiting" and "red scare" tactics of Senator Joseph McCarthy in the 1950s.

Counts was active in American politics. He served as chairman of the American Labor party from 1942 to 1944. In 1944 he helped to launch the Liberal party of New York. In 1952 the Liberal party nominated him as its candidate for United States senator. In this campaign he attacked the policies of Senator Joseph McCarthy and the tactics of McCarthyism as being destructive of American democratic processes and the freedom of individuals.

Counts, the Scholar

Being a man of many talents, Counts was an academic scholar and political activist as well as an educational philosopher and policymaker. As a scholar, he was a prolific author. Beginning his scholarly career under Judd's direction, Counts wrote his doctoral dissertation on "Arithmetic Tests and Studies in the Psychology of Arithmetic." In 1922, in *The Selective Character of American Secondary Education*, he continued to use the survey and sampling techniques associated with the scientific movement in education, but was already beginning to move to broader social issues.[14] Counts's *The Selective Character of American Secondary Education* bore the imprint of his earlier study with Judd and Small. The methodology was that of the scientific school of educational research, which sought to base conclusions

---

[14]George S. Counts, *The Selective Character of American Secondary Education* (Chicago: University of Chicago Press, 1922).

on quantitative and statistical evidence. Counts's conclusions, though numerically derived, had broad sociological implications in that he found the publicly supported high school was serving the needs of the upper socioeconomic classes.

In *The Social Composition of Boards of Education*, 1927, Counts combined empirical research and social analysis to examine the domination of school boards by business interests.[15] He concluded that public educational policy was often formulated according to the special interests of school board members. Because of their members' favored socioeconomic position, school boards were generally conservative in social policy and resistant to social change.

Counts wrote *School and Society in Chicago*, 1928, which examined the Chicago public school system in relationship to that city's social, political, and economic forces.[16] In particular, he investigated the dismissal of the superintendent of schools, William McAndrews, under pressure from Mayor William Hale Thompson. Using a campaign that accused McAndrews of being pro-English, Mayor "Big Bill" Thompson had enlisted the support of Irish and other ethnic groups to force Superintendent McAndrews from office. An even larger thesis that emerged from Counts's study of organized education in Chicago was that school systems were not isolated from, but were intimately related to, social, political, and economic issues.

Counts's *Secondary Education and Industrialism*, the Inglis Lecture of 1929, disclosed a theme that would become central in his social and educational theory.[17] The industrial revolution had unleashed not only economic but also social and political forces whose impact was just beginning to be realized in education. In fact, Counts saw the industrial revolution as marking a great watershed between two radically different kinds of civ-

---

[15]George S. Counts, *The Social Composition of Boards of Education* (Chicago: University of Chicago Press, 1927).

[16]George S. Counts, *School and Society in Chicago* (New York: Harcourt, Brace and Co., 1928).

[17]George S. Counts, *Secondary Education and Industrialism* (Cambridge: Harvard University Press, 1929).

ilization. Written on the eve of the Great Depression, the publication of *Secondary Education and Industrialism* marked Counts's emergence as a national figure in educational theory. His broad theme held economic and social as well as educational implications. Counts's emphasis on the rise of industrial society was a theme that remained constant throughout his long career.

Counts's *The American Road to Culture*, 1930, an interpretive history of American education, located the American public school in its broad social and cultural context.[18] Generally, books on American educational history had concentrated on the school as an institution and on schooling as a process that was relatively insulated from social forces. Counts, however, was a broad contextual thinker who located the school in its historically evolving social, political, and economic contexts. Even as the school was a potent agency of enculturation and formal education, Counts remonstrated that Americans often had an immature and naive faith in organized education's power to solve all sorts of social, personal, and political problems. Counts persistently held that organized education, or formal schooling, was but one of many educative forces in the United States.

In 1932 Counts issued his well-known and provocative challenge to American educators when he asked, *Dare the School Build a New Social Order?*[19] With this small book, which grew out of his earlier "Dare Progressive Education Be Progressive?," Counts entered his most pronounced ideological stage.[20] He was now using educational theory as a rationale for particular social and political policies and programs. His question, which emerged in the climate of the economic crisis of the early 1930s, also had a relevance beyond that troubled decade.

Counts's *The Social Foundations of Education*, a volume in the series produced by the American Historical Association's

---

[18]George S. Counts, *The American Road to Culture: A Social Interpretation of Education in the United States* (New York: John Day Co., 1930).

[19]George S. Counts, *Dare the School Build a New Social Order?* (New York: John Day Co., 1932).

[20]George S. Counts, "Dare Progressive Education Be Progressive?," *Progressive Education* 9 (April 1932): 257-63.

Commission on the Social Studies, appeared in 1934.[21] As the commission's research director, Counts began his long friendship and association with Charles A. Beard. *The Social Foundations of Education* revealed Counts's recognition of the impact of social change on education. He endorsed educational policies that would contribute to social planning, economic coordination, and "democratic collectivism."

When Counts's *The Prospects of American Democracy* was published in 1938, John Dewey commented: "Any one assessing the prospects for democracy in this country must reckon with this book as a great asset on the favorable side, if only it is widely read and studied."[22] This book was Counts's most radical ideological statement on American society and education. Written in the midst of the Depression of the 1930s, Counts's rhetoric demonstrated his fear of the rise of an "economic aristocracy." While he maintained an essentially experimentalist social orientation, Counts urged creation of a collective democracy to sustain the American democratic system in this critical period of its history.

From 1931 to 1937, Counts was senior editor of *The Social Frontier*, a journal of commentary and criticism on the great social issues of the day. This journal was a platform for the social, political, and educational views of such leading American scholars as John Dewey, Charles Beard, William Kilpatrick, Merle Curti, and others.

The Schools Can Teach Democracy, 1939, published at the outbreak of war in Europe, and *The Education of Free Men in American Democracy*, 1941, appearing in the year of American entry into that war, revealed Counts's complete rejection of both the extreme political Right and Left.[23] In these books he voiced

---

[21]George S. Counts, *The Social Foundations of Education* (New York: Charles Scribner's Sons, 1934).

[22]George S. Counts, *The Prospects of American Democracy* (New York: John Day Co., 1938).

[23]George S. Counts, *The Schools Can Teach Democracy* (New York: John Day Co., 1939) and *The Education of Free Men in American Democracy* (Washington: National Education Association, 1941).

his opposition to European totalitarian movements and let it be known that he considered them negative models for American social, political, and educational development.

Education and American Civilization, 1952, was Counts's most mature, comprehensive, and reflective work on American civilization.[24] Like his earlier *The Prospects of American Democracy*, *Education and American Civilization* was broad in scope and general in interpretation. Expressed in more dispassionate language than the book of the 1930s, *Education and American Civilization* presented a humanistic panorama of American culture and education. Ultimately, these analyses of American civilization revealed a basic consistency in Counts's thought. American civilization, he said, rested on the democratic heritage that was born of the frontier freehold. The great transformation in American, as well as in world civilization, was produced by the emergence of a technological order of life. The American challenge was that of creating a revitalized and reconstructed democracy that could function and give order to a technological society. It is Counts's response to this challenge that is the subject of this book. For Counts, the challenge was a continuing one that he attempted to answer in the years of the Great Depression and in the decades that followed until his death in 1974.[25]

---

[24]George S. Counts, *Education and American Civilization* (New York: Teachers College, Columbia University, Bureau of Publications, 1952).

[25]Other books of Counts are: *Education and the Promise of America* (New York: The MacMillan Co., 1946); *Educacao para uma sociedade de homens livres na era tecnologica* (Rio de Janeiro: Centro Brasileiro de Pesquisas educacionais, 1958); *Khrushchev and the Central Committee Speak on Education* (Pittsburgh: University of Pittsburgh Press, 1959); *Education and the Foundations of Human Freedom* (Pittsburgh: University of Pittsburgh Press, 1962). Lawrence J. Dennis and William E. Eaton, eds., *George S. Counts: Educator for a New Age* (Carbondale: Southern Illinois University Press, 1980), provides an essay on Counts's professional life and carefully selected excerpts from his major writings.

Chapter 2

The Depression of the 1930s:
An Educator Reacts to Crisis

George S. Counts's concept of American civilization grew out of his boyhood experience as a son of America's middle border; his exposure to the ideas of such pragmatic scholars as Dewey and Beard; his study of Soviet culture and education; his long career as an educational theorist; and his active involvement in politics. His view of American life and institutions was always dynamic. Within the continuum of his own experience, Counts saw the Great Depression as a catalyst that moved him from pure educational research and theory to the broader and more action-oriented position of political and social ideology. Chapter two examines the impact of the 1930s economic Depression on the formulation of Counts's theory of American civilization.

The period after World War I was a time of great unease in Western culture. When the celebrations had quieted in the capitals of the victorious allies, the victors were uncertain as to what had been won and what had been lost. World War I marked the demise of the old order and the entry of Western civilization into a state of economic, political, and social dislocation and profound cultural transition. Outwardly, much of the old order had perished with the victims of the battlefield, but remnants of a decaying social order survived in obsolescent institutional patterns and values. These residues of a time past impeded humankind's adjustment to a new industrialized and technological social order.

Since the onset of the industrial revolution, the winds of change had been sweeping the Western world. The twin forces of science and industry, wed in technology, had stimulated rapid means of communication and transportation. Great urban centers of population mushroomed. With modernization came social and psychic dislocation and disintegration of accustomed social mores. The First World War and the revolutions following in its wake had accelerated the disintegration of the old social order. Although a transformation of values, beliefs, and mores was needed, confused Western leaders lacked the statesmanship needed to solve the problems of modern life.

Confusion of the Depression Period

During the 1930s, Western civilization plummeted into an economic crisis of unprecedented depth, the Great Depression. The vague atmosphere of social and psychological dislocation after World War I gave way to the very concrete problems of mass unemployment, malnutrition, strife, and despair. The hopes cherished by Woodrow Wilson for a world governed by law turned to ashes as the world was not made safe for democracy but rather for tyranny. Faced with the choice between liberty or bread, starving people chose bread, or even its promise. The bright future promised by parliamentary liberalism dimmed as people sought political salvation elsewhere. In Soviet Russia, the Communist dictatorship of Stalin entrenched itself; in Italy, Garibaldi and Mazzini were forsaken for the Fascist Mussolini; and in Germany, the Nazi Fuhrer Adolf Hitler plunged a knife into the heart of the Weimar Republic. In the United States business and political leaders, overwhelmed by the immensity of the economic crisis, issued muted statements promising prosperity's return. But by 1933, unemployment in the United States had increased from one million in 1929 to almost thirteen million.[1] While some prophesied the coming revolution, demagogues of the Left and Right preyed upon the popular despair.

---

[1]Basil Rauch, *The History of the New Deal, 1933-1938* (New York: Creative Age Press, 1944) 8.

During this time of social and political agony, Americans searched to find an escape from the Depression. Having long placed their faith in peaceful, evolutionary change, many Americans believed the path to progress could be found in a system of popular public education. From the time of the Republic's founding fathers, Americans saw education as the key to national happiness, security, and prosperity. Horace Mann, Henry Barnard, and William Harris—all leaders of American popular education—had promised progress through a populace enlightened by tax-supported public school systems. But in the difficult Depression years, many Americans felt that they had been misled. While a few disillusioned persons rejected the democratic system, others began to examine, to search for, and to formulate a new social philosophy to redeem the promise of American life.

One of these restless men was the educator-scholar George Sylvester Counts. Devoted to the American democratic heritage, he urged educators to act not simply like schoolmasters, but rather like statesmen. In his mind, the educator who sought to formulate educational policy during a time of profound cultural transition needed the statesman's vision. Such a statesmanlike perspective would come only as educational leaders critically evaluated their culture in terms of the realities of a rapidly emergent technological society.

Until the time of the Depression, Counts had devoted his scholarly energies to more limited educational problems. Turning from the more precisely defined pedagogical investigations associated with the scientific movement in education, he began critically to study American educational institutions in their historical, sociological, and philosophical dimensions. As research director of the Commission of the American Historical Association on the Social Studies, Counts worked with such distinguished scholars as Charles E. Merriam, Charles A. Beard, Avery O. Craven, and Jesse H. Newlon to examine the role of social studies and education. In *The Social Foundations of Education,* Counts began with the statement:

The historical record shows that education is always a function of time, place, and circumstance. In its basic philosophy, its social objectives, and its programs of instruction, it inevitably reflects in varying proportions the experiences, the conditions, and the hopes, fears, and aspirations of a particular people or cultural group at a particular point in history.

Education as a whole is always relative, at least in its fundamental parts, to some concrete and evolving social situation.[2]

For Counts, educational policies and programs did not emerge from an isolated inner logic, but rather flowed from the experience and needs of a particular society at a specific historical moment. As he wrote these words in the midst of the Great Depression, Counts shared the frustrations and anxieties of a people who found their dreams of prosperity suddenly turned into a nightmare of rising unemployment, stagnation, and for many, near starvation. But most of all, he feared the growing lack of faith in American democracy itself.

Counts believed that humankind was living in an age of crisis engendered by pervasive technological change. The severity of the Depression had removed discussions of technological change from the academic seminar and had brought them into the life of every American. No longer merely theoretical, the crisis manifested itself vividly in breadlines, idle factories, and the faces of the jobless searching hopelessly for work. In April 1932, Counts challenged his colleagues in American education to take responsibility in the crisis:

> Here is a society in which a mastery over the forces of nature, surpassing the wildest dreams of antiquity, is accompanied by extreme material insecurity; in which dire poverty walks hand in hand with the most extravagant living that the world has ever known; . . . in which breakfastless children march to school past bankrupt shops laden with rich foods gathered from the ends of the earth; in which strong men by the millions walk the streets in a futile search for employment

---

[2]George S. Counts, *The Social Foundations of Education* (New York: Charles A. Scribner's Sons, 1934) 1.

and, with the exhaustion of hope, enter the ranks of beaten men.[3]

By 1933 the army of unemployed Americans was approaching thirteen million wage earners. As agricultural prices plummeted, farm foreclosures rose to new heights. Business, industry, finance, and agriculture reeled under the intense economic pressure. Schools, like other American institutions, suffered from financial retrenchment. Eleven thousand teachers were out of work in New York City; eighty-five percent of Alabama's schools were closed; the wages of Chicago teachers were $28,000,000 in arrears.[4]

The economic crisis caused some Americans to doubt the efficacy of established democratic political processes and to look to a new order based upon Fascism or Communism. Others questioned the value of the American educational system, and wondered who was responsible for its apparent failure.

Many Americans who blamed the business leadership for the coming of the Depression, believed that the machinations of Wall Street speculators had produced the Crash and the ensuing economic crisis. Those who took a more ideological position attributed the Depression to the failure of capitalism. Some alleged that American schools had failed to prepare the people to meet the challenges of industrial society. Fearing that Americans had lost their faith in public education, Edgar W. Knight, the educational historian, wrote that the critics of American education denounced the schools as aimless and ineffective.[5]

Traditionally, many leaders of public education had boasted of the schools' capacity to solve all kinds of social, political, and educational problems. Such "captains" of education as William Torrey Harris and Nicholas Murray Butler had associated the

---

[3]George S. Counts, "Dare Progressive Education Be Progressive?," *Progressive Education* 9 (April 1932): 259-60.

[4]Merle Curti, *The Social Ideas of American Educators* (Patterson NJ: Littlefield, Adams, and Co., 1959) 576.

[5]Edgar W. Knight, *Education in the United States* (New York: Ginn and Co., 1934) 577.

growth of American public schooling with the rise of the business corporations. Often, school administrators were allied with "captains of industry." As far back as Horace Mann and Henry Barnard, educational leaders had claimed that publicly supported schools could prevent labor unrest, strikes, anarchy, and revolution.[6] The progressive historian, Merle Curti, commented that the educators' initial reaction to the Depression revealed great confusion, the absence of a guiding philosophy, and a lack of policies to cope with the crisis. Although dismayed by the collapse of prosperity since the 1920s, Curti believed that educators still hoped to continue their traditional alliance with the leaders of industry and business.

The Depression weakened the traditional alliance between businessmen and educational administrators. Businessmen, caught in the financial pressure of the Depression, urged slashing school appropriations, reducing teacher salaries, and general fiscal retrenchment. During the 1932-1933 school year, reduced educational expenditures had deprived nearly one-third of a million children of the opportunity to attend school.[7] Thus the early 1930s revealed a widespread confusion as businessman, laborer, farmer, politician, and educator denied responsibility and looked for a scapegoat in the person of the other.

To observers of the social scene such as George Counts, the Depression, a symptom of a more serious crisis, required more than a meaningless hunt for scapegoats and villains. Namecalling and accusations would not solve the crisis that Counts believed was deeply rooted within the social fabric. Counts said:

> In speaking of the crisis, however, I would not confine the attention to the months that have passed since October, 1929. I would go back a generation, and even more, and bring into the picture those international rivalries that led to the Great War. Also, I would give a large place to the war itself and to the revolutions that followed in its wake. But I would place far

---

[6]Curti, *Social Ideas*, 577.

[7]Avis D. Carlson, "Deflating the Schools," *Harper's Monthly Magazine* 167 (November 1933): 499.

greater emphasis on those advances in science and technology that have profoundly altered the foundations of human relations.[8]

To Counts, the merging forces of science and technology had altered human social and institutional relationships as they produced an industrial, interrelated, and interdependent society. He contended that American institutions and values lagged far behind the nation's material inventiveness. Counts argued that by clinging to an outmoded individualism, American society had not developed the planning and coordination needed for social progress and integration. In *Dare the School Build a New Social Order?*, Counts claimed:

> The growth of science and technology has carried us into a new age where ignorance must be replaced by knowledge, competition by cooperation, trust in providence by careful planning, and private capitalism by some form of socialized economy.[9]

Conflict in American Political Ideologies

According to Counts's analysis, deep conflicts existed in American life. On the one hand, defenders of the status quo glorified "rugged individualism" as the foundation of the American system of private enterprise capitalism. In opposition, Counts contended that technologically produced economic interdependence required collective planning, policies, and programs. The contradictions in American life were most apparent in the pronouncements of the major political leaders of the United States.

Although American political campaigns frequently are based on contradictory and inconsistent generalizations, the issue of

---

[8]George S. Counts, "Secondary Education and the Social Problem," *School Executive Magazine* 51 (August 1932): 499.

[9]George S. Counts, *Dare the School Build a New Social Order?* (New York: John Day Co., 1932) 48.

individualism versus collectivism was clearly stated by Herbert Hoover and Franklin Roosevelt. Herbert Clark Hoover, president of the United States from 1929 to 1933, a disciple of enlightened economic individualism, saw individual liberty as the genius of American life; curbs upon individual freedom would destroy the American system. For Hoover, individualism produced progress. Proclaiming his belief in the individualism of "the American System," Hoover stated:

> It is founded on the conception that only through ordered liberty, through freedom to the individual and equal opportunity to the individual will his initiative and enterprise be summoned to spur the march of progress.[10]

In Hoover's view, American society was composed of individuals, free and autonomous. Through ability and ambition, certain gifted individuals rose to positions of leadership in society. Individual freedom encouraged as many voluntary associations as were necessary and permitted such associations to be dissolved when they had accomplished their purposes. In attacking the proposed New Deal of his political opponent, Franklin Roosevelt, Hoover expounded on the spirit of true liberalism, which he said created free men and did not seek to regiment them:

> It is a false liberalism that interprets itself into Government operations of business. Every step in that direction poisons the very roots of liberalism. It poisons political equality, free speech, free press, and equality of opportunity. It is the road not to liberty but to less liberty. True liberalism is found not in striving to spread bureaucracy, but in striving to set bounds to it. True liberalism seeks all legitimate freedom first in the confident belief that without such freedom the pursuit of other blessings is in vain. Liberalism is a force truly of the spirit proceeding from the deep realization that economic freedom cannot be sacrificed if political freedom is to be preserved.[11]

---

[10]Herbert C. Hoover, *Addresses Upon the American Road, 1933-1938* (New York: Charles Scribner's Sons, 1938) 3-4.

[11]Ibid., 17.

Hoover determined to resist any suggestion of a "planned economy" or a "collectivistic order." For him, a planned economy meant the centralization of power in the hands of the executive branch of the federal government, administered and perpetuated by an enormous federal bureaucracy. A planned economy was an attempt to crossbreed socialism, Fascism, and free enterprise.[12] Such a mixture, for Hoover, was unthinkable and unworkable if the American System were to be preserved.

Clearly, for Hoover, a curtailment of economic individualism in the "planned economy" of a "collectivistic order" would restrict individual freedom and liberty. Holding economic liberty and personal freedom to be reciprocal, Hoover expressed the philosophy of many American businessmen and the thinking of the Republican party. If Hoover were correct, then Counts was wrong. If the function of education were to express the ideals of a given society at a given time in history, should it not then express the individualistic liberalism embodied in Hoover's American System?

Hoover's successor to the presidency, Franklin D. Roosevelt, offered a political alternative in his New Deal. Based on relief and recovery from economic depression and reform of the system, the New Deal recognized interdependency in American life. Legislation was enacted to aid the recovery of agriculture, finance, industry, business, and labor. Although he felt the New Deal lacked comprehensive planning, Counts believed Roosevelt was moving in the right direction. In *The Prospects of American Democracy*, 1938, Counts quoted from Roosevelt's Second Inaugural Address in 1937 to illustrate the tragic effects of unbridled individualism upon the mass of the population:

In this nation I see tens of millions of its citizens—a substantial part of its whole population—who at this very moment are denied the greater part of what the very lowest standards of today call the necessities of life. I see millions of families trying to live on incomes so meager that the pall of family

---

[12]Herbert C. Hoover, *The Memoirs of Herbert Hoover: The Great Depression, 1929-1941* (New York: MacMillan Co., 1952) 354.

disaster hangs over them day by day. . . . I see one-third of a nation ill-housed, ill-clad, and ill-nourished.[13]

For Counts, these millions of "ill-housed, ill-clad, and ill-nourished" Americans posed the immediate problem for American democracy. It was the very individualism prized by some as the necessary ingredient of the American System that Counts felt to be the cause of its own destruction. Roosevelt called this unregulated individualism into question when he stated:

> I believe in individualism. I believe in it in the arts, the sciences, and professions. I believe in it in business. I believe in individualism in all these things—up to the point where the individualist starts to operate at the expense of society. The overwhelming majority of American businessmen do not believe in it beyond that point. We have all suffered in the past from individualism run wild. Society has suffered and business has suffered.[14]

Counts was a leader among progressive educators who urged that social planning be made an integral part of American educational theory and practice. Roosevelt's Second Inaugural Address in many ways echoed the words of Counts. Controls needed to be established over an interdependent economic system. Science needed to be brought to the service of men. Roosevelt found that only through government could the interrelated problems of a complex society be solved:

> Repeated attempts at their solution without the aid of government left us baffled and bewildered. For, without that aid, we had been unable to create those moral controls over the services of science which are necessary to make science a useful servant instead of a ruthless master of mankind. To do this we

---

[13]George S. Counts, *The Prospects of American Democracy* (New York: John Day Co., 1938) 49-50.

[14]*Nothing to Fear: The Selected Addresses of Franklin D. Roosevelt, 1932-1945*, ed. B. D. Zevin (Cambridge MA: Riverside Press, 1946) 68.

knew that we must find practical controls over blind economic forces and blindly selfish men.[15]

The philosophy of economic individualism in Hoover's American System was diametrically opposed to the policy of economic planning suggested by Roosevelt's New Deal. Both of these conflicting philosophies embodied the hopes, aspirations, and ideals of the American people. However, both required a different approach in educational philosophy and its program. George Counts believed that American educators had to choose between these conflicting ideological viewpoints. He urged educators to abandon ideological neutrality and to take a stand for a well-grounded and cooperative social order.[16]

The Challenge to Education

Although recognizing the Depression as an urgent problem, Counts saw it as a symptom of an overall problem generated by technological revolution. Human material inventiveness, stimulated by science and technology, had surpassed social inventiveness. Developed in an age of agrarian individualism, social institutions were unable to cope with the challenge of economic interdependency. Education, too, had lagged behind social change. Educators were still inculcating an outmoded era of individualism. As the speeches of Hoover and Roosevelt revealed, a bifurcation existed in America's attempt to resolve the problems of a transitional age. In the midst of this confusion, the nation struggled along without resolving the dilemma. Counts believed that organized education must help lead the nation from the morass of confusion and depression.

In the early 1930s, Counts pleaded for educational statesmanship. Asking the Progressive Education Association, "Dare

---

[15]*My Friends: Twenty-eight History Making Speeches by Franklin Delano Roosevelt*, ed. Edward H. Kavinoky and Julian Park (Buffalo: Foster and Stewart Publishing Co., 1945) 33.

[16]The Committee of the Progressive Education Association on Social and Economic Problems, *A Call to the Teachers of the Nation* (New York: John Day Co., 1933) 6.

Progressive Education Be Progressive?," he urged these progressive educators to become educational leaders. In 1932 he broadened his appeal to the teachers of the nation in *Dare the School Build a New Social Order?* In 1934 Counts and other like-minded scholars launched a journal, *The Social Frontier*, which was a vehicle of social and educational criticism and reform. In addresses, articles, and books, Counts urged educators to meet the challenge of a technological era.

Impelled by crisis, Counts began to venture into the realm of political ideology. This movement was facilitated by Counts's own relativistic educational philosophy that construed education as a function of particular historic circumstances. As social institutions, schools were intimately and integrally a component of a particular culture. To serve their society, schools had to deal with the problems and issues of the culture that sustained them. According to this philosophical rationale, Counts believed that American education needed to be based on the American cultural heritage. That heritage, however, was not a simple fabric, but consisted of several strands. For Counts, the challenge was in identifying the cultural strands, or elements, that were suited to the technological age.[17]

American civilization, Counts insisted, had to be measured—in terms of its historical, social, political, and economic development—against the demands of the technological age. From this analysis, he believed a viable concept of American democracy could be derived.

> While the principle of historical continuity must be recognized through the acceptance of certain of the more abiding aspirations, ideals, loyalties, and faiths of the American people, the education program conceived must be fashioned in terms of the realities of industrial civilization.[18]

---

[17]George S. Counts, "Presentday Reasons for Requiring a Longer Period of Pre-Service Preparation for Teachers," *Proceedings of the National Education Association* 73 (1935): 694.

[18]George S. Counts, "The Position of the Social Frontier," *The Social Frontier* 1 (January 1935): 30-31.

If the analysis of American civilization produced a viable tradition, then the dilemma posed in the speeches of Hoover and Roosevelt might be resolved. The basic need was to clarify purposes and to reach agreement on the general direction of the Republic. Although technology had created an interdependent world, people could not cooperate unless a community of shared purpose controlled and unified their actions.[19]

Once national directions were established, then Counts believed it possible to formulate an educational philosophy that encompassed both the American democratic tradition and the emergent technological order. In *The American Road to Culture*, 1930, Counts stated that the American educational system still reflected the conditions and aspirations of pioneering and agrarian society, despite the fact that this old order of life had been replaced by a highly integrated technological civilization.[20] By developing a plan to reconstruct the heritage in light of new conditions, educators could provide needed leadership and direction. To accomplish this task, educators had to be committed to a definite course. Too long, said Counts, had educators feigned neutrality as they tried to follow the impossible task of moving down all roads, even opposite ones, at the same time. Educators had to make fundamental choices regarding the course of national destiny. According to Counts:

> Any concrete school program will contribute to the struggle for survival that is ever going on among institutions, ideas, and values; it cannot remain neutral in any firm and complete sense. Partiality is the very essence of education, as it is of life itself. The difference between education and life is that in the former partiality is presumably reasoned and enlightened.[21]

In calling for statesmanship in education, Counts urged educators to adopt a policy-making attitude toward national problems. What George S. Counts proposed in the 1930s was

---

[19]Progressive Education Association, *Call to the Teachers*, 16.

[20]George S. Counts, *The American Road to Culture* (New York: John Day Co., 1930) 8.

[21]Counts, *Social Foundations*, 535.

something new in the history of American education. To some, the proposals were statements of the most dangerous radicalism. To others, they were a rallying point for American democracy.

Chapter three, "Counts's Frame of Reference," will describe his effort to identify the cultural elements that could be used in creating an educational philosophy for American civilization.

Chapter 3

Counts's Frame of Reference

George S. Counts believed that education was always contextual—rooted in the culture of a particular people at a particular time in history. Organized education in the United States was an expression of American civilization. The formulation of an American philosophy of education first required an examination of the American cultural heritage. From such analysis, Counts hoped to identify the cultural foundations upon which to create a philosophy of American civilization and the education that sustained it.

A Civilizational
Philosophy of Education

For Counts, education was rooted in a concept of civilization, and so existed within the contours and met the needs of a particular culture. The major challenge of American educators, he believed, was to identify the vital elements of American civilization and to reconstruct these elements in order to better resolve the problem of modern, technological life in society.[1] Unless it were rooted in a vital tradition, modernization produced social disintegration and personal confusion.

The period of the Great Depression of the 1930s, a time of national confusion and profound economic crisis, exhibited signs

---

[1]George S. Counts, "To Vitalize the American Tradition," *Progressive Education* 15 (March 1938): 245.

of social anxiety and political disintegration. The lack of coordination between production and consumption, massive unemployment, and market breakdown caused many Americans to question seriously the free enterprise economic system and democratic political processes. In Italy, the Italian people had allowed Benito Mussolini to usurp power in return for the promise of political order and the economic stability of a corporate state. Similarly, in Germany many Germans had accepted Adolf Hitler's Third Reich with its promises of a strong and stable government and full employment.

To George Counts, who experienced and commented on the momentous political, social, and economic events of the twentieth century, the rise to power of a Mussolini or a Hitler was but another aspect of the malaise of Western civilization. Germany and Italy had experienced severe and prolonged social, economic, and political crises. The appearance of the European dictators was a sign of Western society's inability to cope with its headlong rush into industrial and technological modernity.

George S. Counts's career as a social and educational theorist spanned the twentieth century. His well-known *Dare the School Build a New Social Order?*, in 1932, commented on the plight and promise of American education in the years of economic depression. It should be remembered, however, that the relevance of Counts's theory of American civilization and education was not limited to that crucial era. His theory of American civilization and education had a broader significance in that he was attempting to deal with the problems of tradition and change within the framework of a society that was undergoing modernization. More than school problems, America's educational problems were social issues that extended to the core of its civilization. What Counts attempted to fashion was the framework for an American *paedeia*, a culture that would be a self-renewing civilization. The beginnings of an American *polis* were located in the traditions of the society. Only as people were influenced and nurtured by a particular tradition did their lives become integrated and effective. Creative human energy was released as individuals identified with a growing and vital tra-

THE EDUCATOR AS SOCIAL THEORIST

dition. If a tradition were disintegrated, then the lives of those who participated in it would also disintegrate.

In such early studies as *The Selective Character of American Secondary Education*, 1922, and *The Senior High School Curriculum*, 1926, Counts had used statistical methods to examine particular problems of American schools. His research in the early 1920s was concerned primarily with such issues as the selection and retention of students in high school and with the organization of the secondary school curriculum. Stimulated by his interest in sociology and history, Counts was moving to a broader and more integrative perspective on American civilization and education.

The economic depression of the 1930s increased Counts's already existing propensity toward a more inclusive, socially oriented view of education. Concurrent with his analysis of American society and education in relation to economic crisis, Counts also had visited the Soviet Union, which was in the midst of its own modernization with the various Five Year Plans. He saw in the Soviet Union a nation that was using its vast natural resources in a planned and determined, but coercive fashion, to achieve industrial and technological modernity.[2] Counts's own predilection for popular and collective planning in the early 1930s was probably influenced by what he saw and heard in the Soviet Union.

Counts predicted that a modernized Russia would become an industrial and technological giant and a potential political threat to Western democracy. The United States's entry into World War II also demonstrated to Counts that education was an instrument of national survival. During the long Cold War of the 1950s, Counts commented on the political relationship between education and society. Then in the 1960s, Counts argued that American society and education needed to control the mil-

---

[2]George S. Counts, "Diary of Auto Tour in Soviet Union" (1929), George S. Counts Papers, Special Collections/Morris Library, Southern Illinois University at Carbondale. Also see George S. Counts, *A Ford Crosses Soviet Russia* (Boston: Stratford Co., 1930), and *The Soviet Challenge to America* (New York: John Day Co., 1931).

itary complex they had created to preserve democracy so that it would not destroy human freedom. He also saw the school as a potent instrument in creating the "Great Society" that was part of President Lyndon Johnson's War on Poverty. This chain of events—economic depression, World War II, Cold War, plans for the "Great Society"—related to Counts's thesis that education as a process is based in the civilization it serves.

In light of the events of the twentieth century, Counts formulated his civilizational philosophy of education, which was a major impetus in his work. According to his interpretation, human freedom derived from human culture, which is the repository of the hopes, aspirations, and values of a people. Only through participating in the cultural heritage did human beings, individually and collectively, shape their destiny. To the extent that culture was valid and based on the realities of life, it was possible for humankind to master the environment and gain freedom.[3] If the goal of education was human freedom, then the transmission of the cultural heritage was a primary educational objective.

According to Counts, any viable conception of the cultural heritage of American civilization in the twentieth century would be based upon two necessary conditions: (1) affirmation of the values embodied in the historic American democratic tradition; (2) recognition of the dominant reality of modern society, the emergence of an industrial and technological civilization.[4] Through an examination of the American cultural heritage, and with an eye to these two necessary conditions, he sought to fashion a dynamic concept of American civilization and a vitalized educational philosophy. He first attempted such an analysis of American civilization in the 1930s in *Dare the School Build a New Social Order?*, 1932, and in *The Prospects of American Democracy*, 1938. After World War II, in *Education and the Promise*

---

[3]George S. Counts, "Theses on Freedom, Culture, Social Planning, and Leadership," *National Education Association Proceedings* 70 (1932): 249.

[4]George S. Counts, *The Prospects of American Democracy* (New York: John Day Co., 1938) 318.

of America, 1946, he called for an inspiring interpretation of American history in terms of the conditions and possibilities of industrial civilization.[5] With *Education and American Civilization*, 1952, he reiterated that the major task facing American society was to develop an enduring concept of civilization.[6]

Before proceeding to a more thorough consideration of Counts's analysis of American civilization, a brief introductory examination of his operational frame of reference is needed. As stated, the democratic heritage and industrial technology were major components in this frame of reference. Democracy was at the core of the American heritage, and industrial technology was the dynamic of the age. Counts stressed the role of economics as a conditioning agent of civilization. The three elements of economic conditioning, the rise of industrial society, and the rejection of totalitarianism provide a point of departure for appraising George S. Counts's theory of American civilization.

Economic Conditioning

The Depression of the 1930s caused many persons to rethink their basic economic conceptions. In the United States, a glutted market and massive unemployment produced widespread skepticism about the traditional economic wisdom of such sacred concepts as economic individualism, the law of supply and demand, and unregulated capitalism. Such questioning was not new, of course. American scholars were familiar with Marx's critique of capitalism and his rejection of the concepts of such classical economic figures as Adam Smith, David Ricardo, and Thomas Malthus. More to the point for Counts than Marxist economic theory were such native American critics of capitalism as Edward Bellamy, Henry George, and Eugene V. Debs. As noted, Counts was also a close associate of Charles A. Beard, the American historian who had written about the political impact of economics on American history.

---

[5]George S. Counts, *Education and the Promise of America* (New York: MacMillan Co., 1946) 103.

[6]George S. Counts, *Education and American Civilization* (New York: Teachers College, Columbia University, Bureau of Publications, 1952) 58.

Charles A. Beard and Counts developed a scholarly collaboration and deep personal friendship as a result of their association in the American Historical Association's Commission on the Social Studies. Throughout the 1930s and early 1940s, Counts and Beard met and corresponded. Beard, the father-figure of the new progressive and pragmatic history, acted in a similar role toward the younger Counts.[7] The historical perspective from which Counts developed his social and educational policies was essentially Beardian.

During the Depression, Counts, like many other theorists, was so impressed by the role of economics on culture that he could be identified as a proponent of the theory of economic conditioning. His view of the role of economic forces in shaping social and political life resembled Beard's economic interpretation of history rather than Marx's dialectical materialism.[8] Counts's concept of economic conditioning saw economic forces as a powerful causative agency in shaping human history. Unlike Marx's economic determinism, economic conditioning emphasized the role of human preferences in choosing among cultural alternatives. Counts, essentially an instrumentalist, simply did not see history as the product of a predetermined dialectic as did Marx. While he found that human choices were conditioned by a particular environmental and cultural framework, Counts rejected the view that historical processes were blind to human choice. Counts contended human beings in history are "neither wholly bound nor wholly free" and that life, "though always conditioned, is never fated."[9]

Counts observed that American democracy itself had been conditioned by historical economic processes. The landowning, freehold farmers of early nineteenth-century America had cre-

---

[7]Counts/Beard Correspondence, George S. Counts Papers. Also see Lawrence J. Dennis and William E. Eaton, *George S. Counts: Educator for a New Age* (Carbondale: Southern Illinois University Press, 1980) 7.

[8]For Beard's interpretation of the role of economic forces on history, see: Charles A. Beard, *Economic Origins of Jeffersonian Democracy* (New York: MacMillan Co., 1927), and *The Economic Basis of Politics* (New York: Alfred A. Knopf, 1934).

[9]Counts, *Prospects*, 76.

ated the democratic values of independence, equality, and freedom. Scorning class pretensions, the freehold farmer gloried in the worth and dignity of the common man. Based on the origins personified by the freehold farmer, economic democracy soon provided a material base for popular government in the United States during the Jeffersonian and Jacksonian eras.[10] Sharing Beard's emphasis on an economic interpretation of history, Counts viewed the struggle for American independence as the result of economic conflicts between Britain and her North American colonies. The American Civil War he saw as a battle between two groups of common men both enlisted to fight for rival aristocracies. The Southern slaveholding aristocracy enlisted white freeholders, while the rising Northern industrial aristocracy enlisted Northern and Western farmers. When viewed in terms of the modernization process, the Northern states were clearly seeking to extend an industrial economy. Tied to an archaic economic system, the Confederate states sought to preserve the obsolete slavery system from extinction.[11]

In Counts's view, after the Civil War the forces of industrialism dominated American life. Despite agrarian opposition such as populism, the domination of the industrial corporation transformed the economic foundations of American life and society. This revamping of the instruments and organization of production reduced the role of human labor and advanced mechanical power. The effects of industrialization in the United States were not limited to the economic realm, but were dynamic and extended to the noneconomic social and cultural areas of American life. Since economic transformation had repercussions for art, government, morals, and religion, a comprehensive philosophy of education spanned the entire range of life. More specifically, labor, income, property, leisure, recreation, sex, family, government, public opinion, race, nationality, war, peace, art, and aesthetics had to be examined by educational leaders.[12]

---

[10]Ibid., 79.

[11]Ibid., 35-38, 70.

[12]George S. Counts, "Dare Progressive Education Be Progressive?," *Progressive Education* 9 (April 1932): 262.

Although critics charged him with subordinating spiritual values to material ones, Counts argued that liberation from materialism could be achieved only by recognizing the importance of the economic factor. The American people were overly absorbed in the struggle for food, clothing, wealth, and property because the economy was not rationally ordered. Only after achieving material security through rational economic controls could spiritual values be cultivated.[13]

Counts's editorials in *The Social Frontier*, focusing attention on class struggle in the United States during the Depression period, cited the existence of gross inequalities in wealth, income, and power.[14] To secure more favorable conditions for the working population, educators were to ally with organized labor.

The economic crisis of the 1930s produced an era obsessed with economics, and Counts certainly shared that climate. In speaking of "economic aristocracy" and "class struggle," his language took on a radical tone that was not common to educators. After the Depression, the importance given to economic factors lessened in his social and educational theory, even though he continued to believe that a sound economy was basic to democracy. In *Education and American Civilization*, 1952, Counts stated, for example, that a stable economy, full employment, and production were fundamental to political liberty. The historic task remained to maintain both economic stability and political liberty.[15]

Rise of Industrial Civilization

As he worked to construct a viable concept of American civilization, Counts was deeply impressed by the rise of an industrial and technological society that was for him the dominant emergent reality of the twentieth century. For him, the crucial

---

[13]George S. Counts, *The Social Foundations of Education* (New York: Charles Scribner's Sons, 1934) 531.

[14]George S. Counts, "Teachers and the Class Struggle," *The Social Frontier* 2 (November 1935): 39-40.

[15]Counts, *Education and American Civilization*, 19.

problem facing American civilization was to effect a cultural reconstruction that would preserve the democratic ethic within the framework of industrialized society.

In *Secondary Education and Industrialism*, 1929, Counts began to assess industrial civilization. In Counts's view, the invention of the machine as an instrument of production affected human life at every level. Industrialization produced a tendency to occupation differentiation, increased coordination, and greater productive efficiency. Industrial society produced a culture of enormous complexity in which the intimate personal relationships formed in the communities of small-town and rural America had been superseded by predominately functional and impersonal relationships.[16] The processes of modernization had produced an urban, mobile, and technological society in which the task of organized education was to develop, organize, and transmit the knowledge needed to manage this vast network of relationships.

The rise of industrial civilization created great tensions for American civilization. In responding to these tensions, Counts believed that American civilization had two alternatives: (1) it might drift aimlessly on a sea of unregulated individualism and hope that the slow operation of economic forces could bring about adjustment; (2) it could formulate a social and educational policy that attempted a fundamental reconstruction of American culture.[17] In urging fundamental cultural reorganization, Counts formulated a policy to use technology for democratic ends, to preserve individual integrity within a cooperative society, and to achieve efficient and popular control of an intricate and complex social and economic mechanism.[18] The overriding political and educational task required creation of a civilizational philosophy for the emergent American industrialized society. At the heart of this philosophy, Counts envisioned a synthesis of democracy and industrialism.

---

[16]George S. Counts, *Secondary Education and Industrialism* (Cambridge: Harvard University Press, 1929) 9.

[17]Ibid., 64.

[18]Counts, *Prospects*, 320.

The Democratic Commitment

Counts was convinced that a philosophy for American civilization and education should be based on the democratic ethic developed in the American historical experience. During the 1930s and 1940s, totalitarian movements of both the extreme political Left and Right had viciously attacked the democratic middle way. While the Depression had paralyzed economic life in the Western democracies, the Communist party under Stalin's dictatorship had industrialized the Soviet Union with a series of Five Year Plans. The Fascists in Italy and the Nazis in Germany had promised to eradicate both unemployment and sentimental bourgeois democratic ideals. Totalitarianism was not just a European phenomenon. Native antidemocrats, feeding upon popular unrest, attracted followers in the United States. Believing that the democratic ethic needed to be reasserted positively rather than defensively, Counts made democracy a necessary condition in any reconstruction of American society and education. His theories of society and education rested upon a deep faith in the American democratic ethic.

In *The Prospects of American Democracy*, 1938, Counts made two basic assumptions: (1) democracy was a desirable way of life and society; (2) the American people could preserve and extend the democratic ethic if they so resolved.[19] Never deviating from these basic assumptions, he identified the American heritage with the democratic ethical ideal. In 1934 he wrote that despite disillusionment and changing circumstances, democracy remained the most authentic expression of the American genius.[20] Like John Dewey, Counts did not necessarily identify democracy with particular political forms, but rather saw it as a "point of reference" to be used in creating and reconstructing "all social forms and arrangements."[21]

---

[19]Ibid., 75.

[20]Counts, *Social Foundations*, 509.

[21]Ibid., 30.

Counts commented that the rise of totalitarianism was a response to moral, economic, and political disintegration. The fuhrers, duces, and caudillos promised strong leadership. Despite the march of the various dictators, Counts claimed it was contrary to the historic convictions of the American people that European totalitarian models should be emulated in the United States. He urged a searching analysis of the totalitarian threat when he stated:

> The fact that millions of ordinary men and women in Italy, Germany, and other countries, with our example before them and with some experience of their own with free institutions, seem to have turned deliberately to dictatorship suggests that our record is not without blemish. Anyone viewing the poverty and misery of the lower one-third of our population today, the concentration of economic power and privilege in the hands of a small minority, the chronic condition of economic paralysis and insecurity, and our general inability to deal effectively with the problems of industrial civilization, must concede that our success is highly circumscribed. Yet the eyes of the world are on America today as they were in Washington's time.[22]

Fascist and Nazi totalitarianism directly contradicted Counts's beliefs in the democratic ethic, since they rested on principles of inequality. Hitler's Third Reich furnished an unparalleled example of the consequences that occurred when science and technology were used for inhumane purposes.[23] Organized education demonstrated its power when used by manipulators such as Alfred Rosenberg and Joseph Goebbels to generate mass hysteria and racial hatred. Nazi Germany furnished an example that plainly demonstrated that the forces of technology, science, and schooling were potentially instruments of evil as well as of human benefit.

Although Fascism was overwhelmingly rejected by the vast majority of Americans, some Americans—especially radical in-

---

[22]George S. Counts, *The Schools Can Teach Democracy* (New York: John Day Co., 1939) 10.

[23]Ibid., 6.

tellectuals—found Communism appealing in the 1930s. Counts's perspective on Communism and the Soviet Union was interesting. As discussed, in 1929 he had traveled through the Soviet Union when the First Five Year Plan was being implemented. He was impressed by what appeared to him to be Soviet success with mass and popularly based planning. He tended to contrast Soviet planned coordination with chaotic American individualism.[24] By the late 1930s, Counts was beginning to see the Soviet system as a form of Machiavellian mind control that threatened free peoples. In 1939, 1940, and 1941, Counts led campaigns to wrest control of the American Federation of Teachers from American Communists.

Counts's scholarly interest in Soviet planning by no means indicated that he wanted the Russian experience duplicated in the United States. Rather, Counts viewed the Soviet experiment as a powerful and uncompromising challenge for those committed to political democracy. He warned those sympathetic to the Soviets that the Communist party had repudiated political democracy and established a rigid dictatorship that was as authoritarian as that of the Nazis and Fascists. Those who looked to Russia for guidance, he warned, would eventually meet with severe disillusionment.

Although Popular Front movements of democrats, liberals, socialists, and Communists against Fascism were popular in the late 1930s, Counts warned that the democratic forces could not cooperate with any totalitarian movement or party, however loudly it proclaimed devotion to democracy. The Communist party, in particular, he repudiated as an instrument of popular advance.[25] Democracy had to fashion its own programs of dealing with a world in revolution.

Counts's devotion to democracy was a permanent point of reference in his social and educational theory. In all of his works,

---

[24]George S. Counts, "Education and the Five Year Plan of Soviet Russia," *National Education Association Proceedings* 68 (1930): 10.

[25]George S. Counts, "A Liberal Looks at Life," *Frontiers of Democracy* 7 (15 May 1941): 232.

the democratic ethic rested at the heart of his analysis. His *Education and the Foundations of Human Freedom*, 1962, vividly contrasted the democratic ethic with totalitarianism.[26] Counts's social and educational theory can be seen from the following two referents: (1) the emergent reality of an industrial and technological society; (2) adherence to the democratic ethic and the rejection of totalitarianism. Counts began and ended with these two essential elements. The following chapters will examine the nature of the crisis, the democratic heritage in a technological age, the legacy of economic individualism, and Counts's proposed program of action.

---

[26]George S. Counts, *Education and the Foundations of Human Freedom* (Pittsburgh: University of Pittsburgh Press, 1962) 96-97.

Chapter 4

Crisis Between
Two Civilizations

While the Depression of the 1930s prompted George S. Counts to examine the immediate causes of that economic calamity, his analysis of American civilization had stimulated him to formulate more encompassing generalizations about the Western historical experience. Counts possessed the capacity for formulating global theories and relating these broad designs to immediate social, political, and educational issues. His theory that saw American culture poised in a crisis-generating position between two civilizations was part of a larger historical perspective. Chapter four examines Counts's view of this conflict between two civilizations.

As he worked to formulate a theory of American civilization, Counts became increasingly impressed with the modernizing impact of industrial technology on the United States and its people. Modernization, in the form of industrial and technological efficiency, had generated a great transformation of American life. Since the Civil War, the dominant demographical trend in American life had been to the large city and away from the small town and rural farms. The large factory, with its specialized assembly-line production, had replaced the craftsman's small shop. Property was held in larger and larger aggregates by the industrial and business corporations.

Not only had there been alterations in the average American's residence, occupation, and property, there also was a change in beliefs and values. In many respects, this transition in American attitudes and values was unconscious rather than planned deliberately or explained rationally. It had simply occurred. Counts's analysis of American civilization attempted to examine and explain this great shift from an agrarian and rural society to one that was increasingly industrial, urban, and modern.

From the onset of the industrial revolution, crisis-generating tensions had accumulated as Western society moved from a predominantly agricultural mode of life to the radically different life of an industrialized and technological society. World War I, the rise of dictatorships, the Depression, and World War II were symptomatic of dislocation as Western society struggled to regain equilibrium following its headlong rush into a technological world for which it was unprepared.

In order to formulate a theory of American civilization and education, Counts sought to define precisely the nature of the crisis caused by the transition from an agricultural to an industrialized society. His analysis provided a definition of "transition," a consideration of "cultural lag," a comparison of "old pain economy" and the emerging "pleasure economy," and a survey of areas of conflict and confusion. Finally, he challenged Americans to inquire into and devise programs of concerted action to deal with the problem of cultural transition.

Period of Profound Transition

Counts saw American civilization gripped by a period of profound transition. Chronologically this transition, which began with the industrial revolution of the early nineteenth century, would continue through the twentieth century. From a loose aggregation of relatively self-contained rural households and neighborhoods, the American nation, under the impetus of industrialization, had evolved into a vast society characterized by minute differentiations of structure and function. With its common dependence on a far-flung productive and distributive mechanism, twentieth-century America required an ever-increasing measure of cooperative planning and unified direction.[1]

---

[1]George S. Counts, "Presentday Reasons for Requiring a Longer Period of Pre-service Preparation for Teachers," *National Education Association Proceedings* 73 (1935): 696.

Not only did this great transition affect the material and economic foundations of the United States, it also penetrated into the nonmaterial social and cultural relations of American society. Science, technology, invention, and mastery over nature had advanced far beyond the reconstruction of ethics, morals, and laws. The obsolescence of inherited conceptions of human relationships, the decline of faith in traditional moral and religious doctrines, and the appearance of revolutionary political ideologies and programs reflected the instability of Western society.[2]

Counts wrote, "We live in troubled times; . . . an age of profound change . . . of revolution." He commented that a new civilization, unprecedented in human history, founded on "science, technology and machinery," was emerging. Possessing enormous and extraordinary power, the new technological civilization had the potential of creating a single, great world society.[3]

Counts carefully distinguished between normal change and profound transition. Superficially, normal change was a common occurrence, since any age was transitional, poised between the past and the future. However, this superficial notion of change was predicated on the false assumption that even normal change was purely quantitative and uni-directional.[4] Alterations in the material environment also transformed social life. For example, an increase in the number of material inventions or even their refinement eventually precipitated changes in the nonquantitative or cultural environment.

Therefore, the distinction between normal change and the profound transition that generated social crisis was important. Normal change occurred without seriously disturbing or modifying the bases of social life. He stated that Western society had already experienced two stages and was now entering a third stage of civilization. The first stage was based on the natural

---

[2]George S. Counts, "Orientation," *The Social Frontier* 1 (October 1934): 3.

[3]George S. Counts, *Dare the School Build a New Social Order?* (New York: John Day Co., 1932) 31.

[4]Counts, "Presentday Reasons," 696.

arts of hunting, fishing, and trapping; the second stage depended on the laborious arts of agriculture, animal breeding, and handicrafts. Modern man had now entered a third stage of civilization—industrial society. Although its characteristics and outlines were still undefined, Counts termed this third age one of science, technology, industry, close integration, and extraordinary power.[5]

To examine Counts's distinction between normal change and profound transition, hunting civilizations may be used as an illustration. Within the hunting civilization, life was usually nomadic, as hunters moved and searched for prey. Customs, folkways, and mores clustered about hunting and fishing, the traditional modes of livelihood. Normal change occurred within the hunting economy when inventions and refinements elaborated and perfected traditional modes of life. When the hunter put aside the club as a means of killing his prey and developed the more efficient spear, bow and arrow, and snare, the instruments of the hunting economy changed. Perhaps the use of these more efficient tools eventually provided more food, increased population, or depleted supplies of wild animals. Nevertheless, life patterns remained clustered about the hunt, hunter, and hunted. In this sense, normal change occurred, but it did not precipitate profound transition.

In contrast to the normal changes that occurred within the hunting economy and society, profound transition occurred when the simple hunting community entered an agricultural or pastoral mode of life.[6] The hunter's concerns for fish and game yielded to the farmer's preoccupations with improving domestic plants, stock, and agricultural methods. Inherited customs, folkways, and mores that once centered on the hunt had to be reconstructed to focus on the new agricultural pursuits. This profound transformation effected radical alterations in the so-

---

[5]George S. Counts, "The Meaning of a Liberal Education in Industrial Society," unpublished MS (n.d.) 2-3.

[6]George S. Counts, *The Social Foundations of Education* (New York: Charles Scribner's Sons, 1934) 467.

ciety's institutional life. Upon the completion of this social reconstruction, profound transition gave way to normal change. Once again, material inventions caused the improvement of agricultural life as the pointed stick yielded to the hoe, and the hoe to the plow, and the animal-driven plow gave way to the mechanized tractor. Although these inventions initiated change, the mode of life remained agricultural.

Counts's distinctions between normal and profound change clearly anticipated the various modernization theories that were developed by economists, educators, and other social scientists in the 1960s and 1970s.[7] For example, C. E. Black's definition of modernization resembled Counts's basic interpretation of technologically induced cultural change. According to Black, modernization was the

> process by which historically evolved institutions are adapted to the rapidly changing functions that reflect the unprecedented increase in man's knowledge, permitting control over his environment, that accompanied the scientific revolution.[8]

According to Counts, social change had occurred historically when an alteration had taken place in the material realm, such as when a new instrument of production was invented or developed. In periods of normal change, alterations occurred as minor improvements were added to the basic mode of production. Profound change resulted when a transition of historic proportions occurred in the basic means and modes of production.

Although the example of material invention was used as an illustration, Counts did not confine the cause of profound transition to material inventions or refinements. He found the history of every society marked by periods of relatively rapid and

---

[7]For example, see Robert L. Heilbroner, *The Great Ascent: The Struggle for Economic Development in Our Time* (New York: Harper and Row, 1963); Don Adams and Robert M. Bjork, *Education in Developing Areas* (New York: David McKay Co., 1969).

[8]C. E. Black, *The Dynamics of Modernization: A Study in Comparative History* (New York: Harper and Row, 1966) 7.

profound change. In the past, such periods were ushered in by a great environmental or natural change; the driving power of a dominant personality; varying fortunes of migration, war and conquest; processes of social and political revolutions; the peaceful advance of science, discovery, invention, and thought.[9] Whatever their origin, turmoil, upheaval, discord, and maladjustment characterized these periods of profound adjustment.

Counts found that the United States, as well as the other major Western nations, was experiencing profound cultural transitions as it moved from an agricultural to an industrial civilization. Periods of profound cultural change invariably produced social disequilibrium, which affected human life and institutions. Deliberate efforts were needed to reconstruct American social life and institutions to bring them into harmony with the realities of an emergent technological economy and society. In dealing with the problem of the cultural disequilibrium produced by profound social change, Counts was attempting to create a theory that was a cultural synthesis in that it incorporated the viable institutions, processes, and values of the heritage with new cultural additions. He was in no way a conservative who wanted to preserve the status quo or "turn back the clock" to simpler but happier times. What he wanted to do was largely in the Deweyan sense of reconstructing past experience to meet contemporary problems and challenges.

As one who shared the American progressive or liberal perspective in politics and education, Counts believed that periods of social change were times of potential growth and development for both persons and societies. Like John Dewey, whose experimentalist orientation he shared, Counts believed that the new technological age was problematic for humankind. If human intelligence were used to plan and engineer social change in a deliberately reconstructive manner, humankind could enjoy both the material and cultural rewards of the new technological society.

---

[9]Counts, "Meaning of a Liberal Education," 1.

From a Pain to
a Pleasure Economy

During the Depression of the 1930s, Counts repeatedly emphasized the theme of the "great transition" in American life, which he characterized as a movement from a pain to a pleasure economy. Throughout most of their long history on earth, human beings had lived under the duress of a necessary scarcity of economic goods. Under the privations of a pain or subsistence economy, past civilizations had experienced hardship and want. While life had been insecure for the majority of people, a small elite had enjoyed luxury. Moral codes, religions, and philosophies had evolved that sought to rationalize the pain economy by condemning materialism as a sin of moral dissipation.[10]

In the American historical experience, the generalized themes associated with the Calvinist-Puritan ethic had established moral codes based on the residues of the pain economy. The American Puritans sought to rationalize material gain within the contours of a world view that was theistically ordained. Men of property were those who were foreordained by God to be stewards of society. Predestined by Providence, wealthy individuals were to use their property to increase wealth in order to endow society with religious and educational institutions.

While the Puritans saw wealth as a sign of Providential blessing, they disdained the poor as being excluded from the ranks of the elect. The poor person was condemned to poverty, they believed, because of innate moral weakness and an inclination to evil. These notions of the cause of poverty were deeply ingrained in the American character, having been fixed there by long years of enculturation and schooling. It was well into the twentieth century, during Franklin Roosevelt's New Deal and Lyndon Johnson's War on Poverty, that such a view of eco-

---

[10]George S. Counts, "Some Thoughts on the Organization of an Institute of Social Research at Teachers College," unpublished MS (n.d.) 7.

nomic deprivation was deliberately challenged in the political realm.

The theoretical residues of the pain economy also were expressed in the sociology of the late nineteenth century produced by the popular English sociologist, Herbert Spencer, and his American disciple, William Graham Sumner. Spencerian and Sumnerian sociology, or Social Darwinism, enjoyed great popularity in the United States in both academic and public circles.[11] Social Darwinists saw life as a struggle between the "fittest," who were stronger, more resourceful, and more capable, and the "unfit," who were biologically and sociologically inferior. Because of nature's inexorable laws, the struggle for material life would be won by the "fittest," who were to survive. The unfit, meaning in general the poor, were doomed by natural selection to poverty and eventual extinction.

The impact of both the Protestant ethic and Social Darwinism was to exalt the rugged individual who triumphed over adversity because of a superior ethical nature. Prospering in an unplanned and unregulated *laissez-faire* society, the rugged individualist got ahead by his own initiative. Counts found the American character was formed by ethical conceptions nurtured in the pain economy. The Protestant ethic, social Darwinism, and *laissez-faire* capitalism were still deeply ingrained in the public philosophy despite severe challenges to them in academic circles. These theoretical residues inherited from an earlier age justified poverty, inequality, and a maldistribution of wealth. In the social, political, and educational realm, they impeded rational inquiry and blocked the reconstruction of society that was needed in the emergent technological age.

Counts believed that the time had come for the new pleasure economy of plenty, comfort, and leisure to replace the old pain economy based on scarcity. The American people possessed the technological means and power of producing abundant goods and services. The inability of American society to organize its eco-

---

[11]Richard Hofstadter, *Social Darwinism in American Thought* (Boston: Beacon Press, 1955) 30-50.

nomic system to utilize this productive power was one of the great problems of the age.[12] The Depression of the 1930s stemmed from the failure to order rationally the technological power inherent in the pleasure economy. Although American agriculture and industry produced great abundance, the means of distribution, retarded by an obsolete concept of economic individualism, were unequal to the task of diffusing this wealth to the masses. The Depression, as a specific historical event, and poverty, as a general social phenomenon, were unnecessary in light of twentieth-century industrial and technological realities. In his analysis of America's social and economic transition, Counts determined that the nonmaterial aspects of the culture derived from the pain economy were not adaptable to the economy of plenty. The rise of industrial civilization made imperative a radical rethinking of the entire system of values inherited from an age of toil, poverty, and bitter struggle with the natural elements.[13] Having lived through two civilizations, human beings now verged on a third, technological one.

Cultural Lag

As American civilization moved from a subsistence economy to a technological one, Counts observed that a lag had developed between the material and nonmaterial aspects of the culture. A cultural lag, he wrote, was at the heart of the problem of transition between these two kinds of civilization. Although not unique to Counts, the theory of cultural lag was a crucial part of his analysis of the difficulty in adjusting to the emergent technological order. Counts noted that a cultural lag occurred when human practical and material inventiveness outdistanced moral consciousness and social organization. The American people faced an institutional crisis produced by a series of maladjustments between inherited ideas, values, social practices, and

---

[12]George S. Counts, "A Proposal for Historical and Cultural Foundations at Columbia," unpublished MS (n.d.) 2.

[13]Counts, *Social Foundations*, 507.

ethics on the one hand, and material, scientific, technological, and industrial innovations on the other.[14]

Counts was familiar with William F. Ogburn's study of the influence of inventions and discoveries on social institutions and values. It was Ogburn who suggested that social adaptation lagged behind material innovation. In identifying this time lag, Ogburn wrote:

> The inventions occur first, and only later do the institutions of society change in conformity. Material culture and social institutions are not independent of each other, for civilization is highly articulated like a piece of machinery, so that a change in one part tends to effect changes in other parts—but only after a delay. Man with habits and society with patterns of action are slow to change to meet the new material conditions.[15]

Counts applied the cultural lag theory to the Depression and to other problems. He reasoned that adaptations had proceeded unevenly in the social structure. Science, technology, and inventions progressed more rapidly than political, social, and educational policies. Even within the economic sector, modes of production changed more rapidly than means of distribution. Glutted markets, lack of purchasing power, oversupply and underconsumption, and massive unemployment during the Depression were economic consequences of the cultural lag in social relationships that caused conflicts of interest among groups and classes. Such economic and social disequilibrium severely strained democratic institutions and processes.

A simple example that illustrates the problem of cultural lag can be found in the invention of the automobile. Henry Ford and others who invented the automobile considered it to be a machine-powered vehicle that would facilitate transportation, making it more efficient and less burdensome. Users of the newly

---

[14]George S. Counts, *The Prospects of American Democracy* (New York: John Day Co., 1938) 9.

[15]William F. Ogburn, "The Influence of Invention and Discovery," in Report of the President's Research Committee on Social Trends, *Recent Social Trends in the United States* (New York: McGraw-Hill Co., 1933) 166.

invented automobile at the turn of the century called it a "horseless carriage." The terminology, "horseless carriage," vividly illustrates the cultural lag theory in terms of linguistic adaptation to material invention. Essentially, those who used this phrase viewed the new contraption as a simple means of conveyance that was much like the horse-drawn carriage; but in this case, it lacked the horse.

In terms of socioeconomic realities, however, the automobile was far more than a horseless carriage. It was an invention that was to have far-reaching consequences. First of all, the demand for and the production of automobiles created an enormous industry. The production and sale of automobiles by General Motors, Ford, American Motors, and the other producers in this industry directly affected the economic well-being of the United States, and even of the world economy. As we see today, decline in automobile sales has had severe implications for the American economy. However, the direct relationship that developed between the American automobile industry and the United States's economy was not immediately seen, nor understood, in the years after the automobile's invention. For a time, there was a lag in explaining and comprehending this relationship.

The effects of an invention are cumulative and dynamic in that they impact other social and economic areas. The automobile was capable of moving at speeds and covering distances that were not possible with the horse-drawn carriage. The gravel and dirt roads used for horse-drawn traffic were unsuited to use by the automobile. A great industry arose to construct the concrete and asphalt highways needed by the nation's automobiles.

The chain reaction caused by the invention of the automobile can be pursued still further. With the large-scale production of automobiles and with the massive construction of highways and expressways came needed educational and legal adaptations. In higher education, the specialties of transportation planning and highway engineering developed to design the networks needed to convey the millions of automobiles found on American roads. As safety problems developed, courses in driver training were incorporated in the American high school curriculum. In the legal area, legislation had to be drafted and enacted to regulate the licensing of vehicles, to determine their proper use, and to regulate such matters as safe speeds per hour for certain areas and conditions. The traffic court was developed as a legal institution, with its body of statutes, to deal with violations of the law that governed automobile ownership and use.

The automobile not only had repercussions for the economy, politics, law, and education, it also had consequences for American social life and mores. For instance, the car had tremendous effects on the dating and courtship patterns of American youth. No longer was the sexual behavior of young Americans subjected to the scrutiny of the chaperon. Now the courting couple could escape from the vigilance of the supervising adult. In fact, the meaning of the word "chaperon" changed from that of a person who accompanied the courting couple, to mean adults, usually teachers, who supervised the school prom or dance.

The invention of the automobile also gave Americans great freedom of mobility. Indeed, the United States became a mobile society that was constantly "on-the-go." Tourism, motel chains, and "fast food" became part of American culture. Such words as Holiday Inn, McDonald's, and Kentucky Fried Chicken gained national recognition.

Did the inventors of the automobile who began their tinkering in backyard garages anticipate the great cultural transformation that they would engineer? Did they know that they would be contributing to America's contemporary problems of environmental pollution by emissions of automobile exhaust fumes, or that they would be causative agents in the international energy crisis? Obviously not!

The dynamic and cumulative effects of the invention of the automobile have been illustrated, albeit simply. A similar analysis could be applied to the invention of the contraceptive pill. In terms of man's continued existence on this planet, the invention and use of atomic weapons, nuclear energy, the hydrogen bomb, and intercontinental ballistic missiles pose serious threats. Is it possible that man's reconstructive intelligence can resolve the problems of nuclear weaponry and energy?

As a social and educational theorist, George Counts saw that the cultural lag between material inventiveness and the reconstruction of social institutions, laws, and values was of momentous significance. While education, especially schooling, had the task of introducing the young to their cultural heritage—its language, literature, history, politics, traditions, art forms, and ethics—this introduction could not be restricted to merely preserving the status quo. A dynamic education was needed to make the future citizens of the nation aware of the prospects and problems of American civilization. Above all, it had to demonstrate the effects of material invention and cultural lag on American as well as world society. The task was to prepare competent individuals to devise means of reducing the lag between material invention and the reconstruction of cultural values. Not only must the lag be reduced, Counts argued, but the future had to be planned and directed rationally. In a nuclear world, it was no longer adequate to use a "gunboat" response to international problems.

Referring to the work of Stanley Casson, the English archaeologist-historian, Counts cited Casson's *Progress and Catastrophe* several times in *The Prospects of American Democracy*, 1938. Casson had illustrated the cooperative nature of human survival in the environment by using historical examples from ancient civilizations. Casson attacked Herbert Spencer's "perverted Darwinism" for stressing competition and ignoring the element of cooperation. In supporting his proposal for an Institute for the Study of Historical and Cultural Foundations of American Education at Columbia University's Teachers College, Counts quoted Casson, who said: "When his practical inventiveness ran ahead of his moral consciousness and social organization, then man has equally faced destruction."[16]

Existence of Widespread Confusion

Counts believed that the American political and educational leadership had neglected the problems of cultural transition between two radically different kinds of civilization. Counts found

---

[16]Stanley Casson, *Progress and Catastrophe* (New York: Harper and Brothers, 1937).

that Americans, lacking a clear conception of their historic destiny, had never really applied their energies to formulating a program to achieve the common good.[17] Without this common goal, the American people had not developed the insight and leadership needed to create a "Great Society." Although Americans were theoretically committed to democratic values, the absence of consensus ill-equipped them to apply those values to social, political, and economic problems during a crisis period. This confusion as to means and ends resulted from obsolete social ideas and from superficial and fragmentary knowledge of industrial society. Although many sensed that something was wrong, they were uncertain as to the precise cause of the problem. Counts attempted to dispel this confusion by identifying the major contradictions in American society. He found two philosophies generated in the American historical experience to be in irreconcilable conflict. One was the Hamiltonian-aristocratic concept of a state based upon the interests of a privileged class; the other was the Jeffersonian-democratic concept, resting upon the general welfare.[18] Needless to say, Counts advocated the ascendancy of the Jeffersonian concept.

Counts found that the Depression revealed deep conflicts within the American economy. Basic to those contradictions was the concept that the general welfare was best served by individuals devoted to guarding and advancing private interests. According to this concept, the nation's natural resources were subject to ruthless exploitation without concern for the needs of posterity; the powerful productive processes of industry were to serve profit interests instead of human needs; human labor was a commodity to be bought and sold. Specifically reflecting on the Depression era, Counts stated that the wages paid to workers were insufficient to allow them to purchase the very products they manufactured. The result was that industrial production

---

[17]Committee of the Progressive Education Association on Social and Economic Problems, *A Call to the Teachers of the Nation* (New York: John Day Co., 1933) 12.

[18]Ibid.

grew more rapidly than effective consumer purchasing power. Referring to political indecisiveness, Counts said:

> Finally as the day of reckoning dawns, the leaders of the nation resort to prayer and incantation, declare that business troubles are psychological, and employing the language of the stock market, appeal to the people "not to sell America short."[19]

Counts found that contradictions existed both in politics and economics. Following the Hamiltonian philosophy, powerful special-interest groups, especially industrial and financial ones, used government as a tool to do their bidding. Through protective tariffs, economic concessions, and financial subsidies, government had encouraged and protected the growth of economic privilege.

Counts found that incongruity existed between science and society. An instrument of extraordinary power, science could be used deliberately to promote the general welfare, but only if rationally directed. Instead of using broad and humane ends, however, special interests had usurped the force of science to narrow and selfish ends. Guarding of trade secrets, suppression of knowledge, consumer exploitation, and misrepresentation had misappropriated a potentially beneficent power into a means for increased private profits. The traditional competitive economy was in irreconcilable conflict with the rationality of science.

The industrial revolution stimulated communication and transportation. The growth of mass media weakened the isolation and self-sufficiency both of the family and the self-contained neighborhood. In modern society, individuals lived in a world of unprecedented complexity that taxed their comprehension. American society lacked a comprehensive and rational plan for using the agencies of mass communication for purposes of enlightenment and understanding. Special-interest groups had usurped the mass media to obscure, confuse, and make personal profit. Although possessed with instruments for creating an informed public, American society did not move toward that end.

_____

[19]Counts, *Social Foundations*, 515.

Counts found aesthetic expression reflected the political, social, and economic confusion as the struggle for profit absorbed productive energies. When the community lost integrity, its great art disappeared and art became a commodity, a cheap product, to be sold for private gain. Art, then, lost its intimate connection with the practical affairs of life and was relegated to leisure time. Eventually, a leisure class monopolized art as a private domain. As a result of this separation from practical life, art was moved to private collections or museums while goods became cheap and shoddy. Instead of using technology to build a beautiful way of life, slums and squalor arose.

Similarly, Counts commented on the deep conflicts in recreation and leisure. Increased productivity and reduction of labor time had increased cultural tensions rather than reduced them. Reduced labor time had come to mean either unemployment or the interruption of income for indeterminate periods of time. The consequent lack of income, generated by periods of unemployment, lowered the public's mental and physical health.[20]

Counts attributed the existence of these conflicts to the persistence of the Hamiltonian ideology in American life. Based upon economic individualism and the quest for profit, inherited concepts nurtured in the pain economy retarded the growth of a genuinely cooperative commonwealth.

After defining the nature of the general problem of cultural transition and citing the major contradictions present in American society, Counts called upon scholars and educators to undertake a bold inquiry that would help Americans to understand their situation. Such an inquiry, he hoped, would encourage basic social reconstruction that was capable of resolving the contradictions of American life. By bringing institutions and values into harmony with the realities of industrial society, the cultural lag would be lessened. The interdependent, collective character of a technological economy required the making of great historic choices. Educators and educational institutions had an important role in determining these historic choices. Evasion of this

---

[20]Ibid., 520-25.

task would place educators on the side of outmoded anarchy and disorder. Counts issued this challenge in *Dare the School Build a New Social Order?*

> I would consequently like to see our profession come to grips with the problem of creating a tradition that has roots in American soil, is in harmony with the spirit of the age, recognizes the facts of industrialism, appeals to the most profound impulses of our people, and takes into account the emergence of a world society.[21]

Throughout his career as educational statesman and philosopher, this challenge of Counts, voiced in 1934, remained the unfulfilled task of American education. He restated the problem of a civilization in the midst of profound transition in his later works, *Education and the Promise of America*, 1946, *Education and American Civilization*, 1952, and *Educacao para uma sociedade homens livres na era tecnologica*, 1958. The nuclear armaments race, with weapons of mass destruction, again illustrated a cultural lag between material invention and rational social control. The overarching task of education remained to close the gap between practical inventiveness and human moral consciousness and social organization.

In his discussion of the concepts of "profound transition," "pain and pleasure economies," and "cultural lag," Counts suggested possible analytical definitions that might be used to study civilization in the throes of crisis. After indicating the theoretical dimensions of the crisis between two civilizations, he turned his attention to a more thorough analysis of democracy and technology, the major components of his theory of American civilization. Chapter five will examine Counts's analysis of the American democratic heritage and the rise of an industrialized technological society.

---

[21]Counts, *Dare the School?*, 39.

Chapter 5

The Democratic
Heritage in a
Technological Age

The need to reconstruct the American democratic heritage to meet the needs of a technological society was a central theme in Counts's analysis of American society. According to his frame of reference, Counts determined that democracy was a desirable way of life and that technology was an emergent reality in an industrialized society. The theoretical task was to formulate a concept of democracy that encompassed this emergent reality. Counts sought to identify the elements upon which to create such a theory by carefully examining the American democratic heritage. To describe the scope of this problem, this chapter examines Counts's analysis of both the American democratic heritage and technology in relation to it.

Roots of the American
Democratic Heritage

Counts embarked on his analysis of American democracy by surveying the conditions prevalent in European civilization at the time of the discovery and exploration of the Western hemisphere. He noted that the discovery, exploration, and settlement of North America coincided with the disintegration of medieval institutions and with the awakening of intellectual life in the great movements of the Renaissance, Reformation, and Enlightenment. Never friendly to medievalism, Counts believed the origins of American civilization were beneficently free of the restrictive institutions and structures of the Middle Ages.

Counts's antipathy to medievalism was not unlike that of other progressive historians and educators who summarily dismissed the Middle Ages as a dark period in human history. These liberating and humanistic forces, conceived in European intellectual theory, were transported to the New World and in the American wilderness took root and flourished. However, in the civilization of America they were not confined merely to theory, but had a practical culmination in the Revolution and the birth of our nation. To Counts, American cultural foundations reflected the following revolutionary tendencies developed in Europe at the time of North America's settlement: (1) the disintegration of the medieval system; (2) the emergence of the middle class; (3) the overthrow of the feudal economy and the growth of capitalism; (4) the rise of parliamentarianism; (5) the disestablishment of the Church.[1]

The absence of an elite social class, surviving from the precapitalistic feudal period, encouraged a more democratic and egalitarian society in the United States.[2] The spirit of the revolutionary era aided the growth of democracy in Britain's North American colonies. Along with this spirit, the North American environment nurtured independent equalitarianism on the frontier and contributed to the achievement of American independence.

Counts found the genesis of the democratic ethic in preindustrial, pre-Civil-War America, where democracy arose among the small landowning, independent, freehold farmers. The source of freehold democracy was economic; in most states it preceded the creation of democratic political institutions. It is worthwhile recalling that Counts believed political democracy derived from economic and social democracy.[3] Abundant supplies of fertile land made the freehold the dominant unit of the rural

---

[1]George S. Counts, *The Prospects of American Democracy* (New York: John Day Co., 1938) 34-35.

[2]George S. Counts, *Education and the Promise of America* (New York: MacMillan Co., 1946) 32.

[3]Counts, *Prospects*, 37-38.

economy in preindustrial agrarian America. Dependent solely upon his own labor, the individual farmer enjoyed social status and economic security. With the exception of the plantation system in the South, the mode of freehold life produced a rough equality of conditions.[4] Easy access to unoccupied land weakened the possibility for the growth of coercive power by a landed aristocracy. Counts cited journals of foreign travelers such as Alexis de Tocqueville to contrast American equality with European inequality and to demonstrate the uniqueness of the American frontier experience.[5]

Counts's analysis of American civilization placed great emphasis on the role that economic forces exercised in the shaping of both social classes and political institutions. Although he fully believed that the origins of American democracy were largely influenced by economics, he also considered it possible that political action could control economic forces.

In charting the evolution of democratic institutions, Counts stated that economic equality occasioned social democracy. Since farming was the major source of livelihood, occupations were generally undifferentiated in preindustrial America. Without occupational differentiation, an equality of occupations and hence of social life prevailed. Counts asserted that the social democracy of preindustrial America demonstrated a strong faith in the common man and antagonism for divisive, artificially contrived social distinctions.[6] In politics, the condition of freehold equality generated popular demands for political equality in the Jeffersonian and Jacksonian movements toward universal suffrage.

In his account of the rise of American democracy from the economic base to a social, and finally to a political level, Counts identified equality as a major element. When he called upon

---

[4]Ibid., 24.

[5]George S. Counts, *The Social Foundations of Education* (New York: Charles Scribner's Sons, 1934) 13.

[6]George S. Counts, *The American Road to Culture* (New York: John Day Co., 1930) 77.

American educators to stand against Fascism in the 1930s and 1940s, Counts stated that democracy rested on an unqualified devotion to the preservation and realization of the essential quality, dignity, and moral worth of all people.[7] This ideal was American civilization's most distinctive and precious quality. Fundamentally, democracy's institutions, processes, and values existed to further the individual's welfare and development. Reaffirming legal and moral equality, all individuals possessed equal rights, liberties, opportunities, and responsibilities.

In part, Counts drew his notion of democracy from the models envisioned by America's early leaders. For Jefferson, a democratic society rested on the proposition that all individuals "are created equal, that they are endowed by their Creator with certain inalienable rights, that among these are Life, Liberty, and the pursuit of Happiness." According to Lincoln, it was a government "of the people, by the people, and for the people"; and to Horace Mann, it was "that form of government and of society which is inspired above every other with the feeling and consciousness of the dignity of man."[8] Counts also found the democratic tradition expressed in the lives and works of such men as Andrew Jackson, Ralph Waldo Emerson, Walt Whitman, Henry George, and John Dewey.[9]

Decline of Economic Democracy

In his writing during the Depression of the 1930s, Counts warned that the democratic ideal was in jeopardy. Although the formal conditions of American political democracy had been extended, its economic underpinnings had gradually contracted. The America of the egalitarian freehold agriculturalist had been replaced by the domination of corporate industries. With the closing of the frontier, the exhaustion of free land, and the

---

[7]George S. Counts, *The Schools Can Teach Democracy* (New York: John Day Co., 1939) 13.

[8]Ibid., 12-13.

[9]The Committee of the Progressive Education Association on Social and Economic Problems, *A Call to the Teachers of the Nation* (New York: John Day Co., 1939) 13.

growth of population, the old economic foundations of democracy had been eroded.[10] Individuals no longer controlled the tools of production; productive property was concentrated in fewer and fewer hands. As economic equality declined, so did social equality. Widespread variations in life styles, specialized occupations, and cultural opportunities had generated significant differences in social and political perspectives. The advocacy of social doctrines of human inequality was based upon economic inequalities crystallizing in America. Such inequalities stimulated some groups to seek establishment in the United States of a "leader principle" similar to that of German Nazism.[11]

Counts found that the historical development of American democracy had experienced three stages: (1) the economic equality of the freehold farmers; (2) the social equality of frontier society; and (3) the political equality of Jeffersonianism and Jacksonianism. It was possible, he warned, that economic inequality would cause social inequality. In a society of great social inequality, political equality would not endure. Counts warned that free government remained free only as long as it rested on free men; men were not freed by government: "They are made free or are enslaved by the conditions under which they live and gain their livelihood."[12]

With the decline of its equalitarian economic and social foundations, Counts feared that the very survival of political democracy in the United States was jeopardized. The American people could not content themselves with past achievements, nor could they rely on an aimless, drifting policy. The great social trends of the contemporary world demanded measures to reconstitute the American democratic tradition. The past with its frontier, free land, and simple agrarian order was no more. In its place a closely integrated, industrial economy was rapidly encompassing the world.[13]

---

[10]Counts, *Social Foundations*, 528.

[11]Counts, *Prospects*, 58.

[12]Ibid., 39.

[13]George S. Counts, *Dare the School Build a New Social Order?* (New York: John Day Co., 1932) 42-43.

In the modern industrial age, Counts believed that the survival of democracy depended on developing new organizational forms. Because industrial life implied cooperative action, the continuance of American democracy rested on the American people's capacity to become more socially concerned and involved with the general welfare. A crucial task of American education was to develop in individuals a devotion to the common good.

Counts did not attempt to define the contours of the society that he envisioned as necessary for the survival of American democracy. Instead of predicting the desired contours of the future society, he relied on the open-endedness of instrumentalism: the American people would shape their own destiny. In fact, Counts wrote that the future of American democracy depended on the ability of the people "to learn from experience, to define the problem, to formulate a program of action, to discover, appraise, and marshal the apparent and latent, the actual and potential resources of American democracy."[14]

Although the pattern of the future American democracy was undetermined—still to be created by the exploration, invention, and experimentation of the American people—Counts suggested a tentative definition in *Dare the School Build a New Social Order?*. Not to be confused with political forms or functions of the Constitution, popular elections, or even universal suffrage, he stated that the most genuine expression of democracy "is a sentiment with respect to the moral equality of men: it is an aspiration towards a society in which this sentiment will find complete fulfillment."[15]

A society in harmony with the American democratic tradition would combat social inequalities and distinctions. It would restore the social equality that produced the American democratic heritage. This reconstructed democracy would, in Counts's words,

> manifest a tender regard for the weak, the ignorant and the unfortunate; place the heavier and more onerous social

---

[14]Counts, *Prospects*, 350-51.
[15]Counts, *Dare the School?*, 40-41.

burdens on the backs of the strong; glory in every triumph of man in his timeless urge to express himself and to make the world more habitable; exalt human labor of hand and brain as the creator of all wealth and culture.[16]

Counts's reconstructed democracy would seek to achieve genuine equality of opportunity for people of all races, religions, and occupations. The paramount concern of this democracy would be the common good of the great masses of the people. No longer would government serve the common man by elevating and refining his life. No mere middle way between the extremes of political Left and Right, the democracy of which Counts spoke was unique, adventurous, and radical. Counts called for a reaffirmation of America's revolutionary tradition when he urged the reborn democracy to

> transform or destroy all conventions, institutions, and special groups inimical to the underlying principles of democracy; and finally be prepared as a last resort, in either the defense or the realization of this purpose, to follow the method of revolution.[17]

It should be apparent that rather than postulating well-defined analytical criteria of democracy, Counts's discussion of the concept of democracy was an expression of faith in the democratic ethic. In summary, four major characteristics of democracy appeared from his analysis of the American tradition. One, his particular concept of democracy was definitely and uniquely associated with the American historical experience. Although he briefly mentioned European antecedents, Counts's concept of democracy was substantively based on American historical foundations. Two, American democracy was not solely political, but was a synthesis of economic, social, and political forces operating within the heritage. Three, equality rested at the roots of democracy. Only in a society of equals could democracy develop and flourish. Any economic, social, or political attempts to sub-

---

[16]Ibid., 41.
[17]Ibid., 42.

vert the egalitarian foundations of American democracy should elicit vigorous opposition from the proponents of democracy. Essentially, democracy expressed the life of the American community. Since the social life of industrialized society was highly organized, the preservation of democracy rested on the ability of the American community to reconstruct its institutional life in harmony with an emergent technological civilization.

De-emphasis of Economics in Counts's Post-Depression Works

After the 1930s Counts's subsequent works continued to emphasize the democratic ethic. In his post-Depression writing, his definition of democracy broadened and matured. In *The Prospects of American Democracy*, 1938, Counts devoted attention to America as the child of the Renaissance, Reformation, and Enlightenment. In the later works, *Education and the Promise of America*, 1946, and *Education and American Civilization*, 1952, Counts expanded the consideration given to the early American heritage as a part of the basic movement of Western civilization. This was done at the expense of the economic factors stressed earlier. In these later works, he called attention to the humanism of the Greeks and the Renaissance scholars. Humanism was a vital intellectual current at the time of the voyages of exploration that led to the discovery of the New World. Counts defined the humanistic spirit as a belief in the possibility of human progress and faith in the ability of man to perfect human institutions.[18]

Counts also gave greater significance to the Judeo-Christian tradition in the American heritage. Historically, the tradition had discernible influence on American civilization, for it proclaimed the supreme worth and dignity of the individual person. All social arrangements and institutions were judged by this precept of equality among all members of society. Although Counts did not urge the acceptance of this faith in its totality, he regarded the emphasis on the dignity of the person to be a

---

[18]Counts, *Education and the Promise*, 82-83.

basic and essential part of the American social creed.[19] The Judeo-Christian tradition thus supplied moral foundations for the democratic ethic.

Counts's later writings provided a more cosmopolitan, humanistic view of the democratic origins of the United States and of the American people. He moved toward a cultural definition of democracy and away from a predominantly economic one. In addition to the increased attention given to the cultural origins of democracy, his later works gave greater emphasis to American political institutions and processes. In *Education and American Civilization*, 1952, Counts argued that democracy could endure only if standards of basic morality were observed in all public relations and in the conduct of all public affairs. The democratic temper placed its faith in methods of enlightenment, persuasion, and peaceful adjudication of differences by legal and orderly processes. He proclaimed that the process of revolution could be institutionalized and conducted without resort to organized violence or civil war.[20]

Throughout his works, Counts continued to emphasize the doctrine of equality of opportunity, which he held was basic for the survival of democracy. The very foundations of freedom would be destroyed if America ever lost the capacity to provide opportunity for the common man. Democracy thrived only in a mobile and progressive society in which security was guaranteed through equal opportunity.

In *Education and American Civilization*, 1952, Counts once again examined the problem of economic distribution in an industrial society. Title to productive property, he said, was held largely by a small class while the great masses of the population depended on employment for a livelihood. Although increasingly heavy taxation, organization of workers, and political legislation had checked the economic elitism of the 1930s, great disparity

---

[19]Ibid., 78, 239.

[20]George S. Counts, *Education and American Civilization* (New York: Teachers College Press, Columbia University, Bureau of Publication, 1952) 283.

of wealth still threatened democratic institutions. Recalling the Depression era, Counts warned that without preventive measures, the United States would eventually experience economic recession or depression. Until a stable economy was created, American democracy remained in danger.[21]

Technology Similar to Scientific Method

For Counts, the essential task was to formulate a social and educational philosophy that was capable of guiding the reconstruction of the democratic heritage to meet the conditions of industrial and technological life. In the first part of this chapter, Counts's interpretation of the American democratic heritage was examined. This section will examine his analysis of industrial civilization, which he looked upon as a product of science and technology. The application of science to the techniques of life had created a new and dynamic cultural force: technology. The harnessing of science to methods of production had accelerated mechanical inventions.

Technology was the dynamic process that had contributed to the rise of modern, industrial society. In Counts's emerging social philosophy, democracy, arising from the American cultural heritage, was to be superimposed on technology so that the process could be directed in the popular interest. Counts's definition of technology as "the art of applying science and mechanics to the various departments of human economy" was simple and straightforward.[22] However, his analysis of technology was marked by complex cultural and material ramifications. Viewing technology as a creative product of cultural evolution, Counts considered it a purposeful process or method of solving problems. As a method for applying knowledge to life, technology had practical and measurable consequences. In addition to being a cultural instrument, technology had an immediate effect on the inventions, discoveries, and products of the material culture.

---

[21]Ibid., 285-86.

[22]Counts, *Social Foundations*, 55.

Counts, who identified thoroughly with Dewey's pragmatic instrumentalism, was committed to using the scientific method as the most efficacious form of problem solving. Scientific knowledge and the scientific method were necessary to the operation of technology and received special analysis in Counts's writings. Like the other pragmatist educators, he saw the scientific method as a process that liberated and used human intelligence to produce dependable and ordered knowledge. Scientific knowledge, because it gave humankind power, control, and freedom, was seen by Counts as the single greatest force moving and shaping the environment in the modern age.[23] Treating science as a method of testing knowledge, Counts further defined it as a "method of organized and critical sense," which consisted of the following steps: (1) the formulation of an idea or hypothesis, growing out of previous experience, knowledge, and thought; (2) the testing of the idea or hypothesis by a process of accurate and adequate observation that employed precise instruments; (3) collection of data and verification or rejection of the hypothesis on the basis of publicly available observed and measured fact.[24] Counts's definition of the scientific method closely resembled John Dewey's "Complete Act of Thought."

Counts found that the method of science, broadly conceived, applied to all areas of life. In its broader range, science might or might not be applied to life in a society that had an industrial base. For example, Nazi Germany and Communist Russia had applied technology to their industrial and military apparatus without applying it to the other areas of life. In Nazi Germany the scientific method was forced to yield to the unscientific racism of Hitler's regime. In the Soviet Union, Marx's dialectical materialism, with its predetermined laws of social change, reigned to the exclusion of an open and experimenting society. When used in a restricted sense as controlled experimentation to achieve material invention, the scientific method has been a necessary condition for the rise of technological societies.

---

[23]Counts, *Education and American Civilization*, 246.

[24]Counts, *Education and the Promise*, 87-88.

Although he emphasized the importance of science, Counts did not believe that science alone encompassed the whole of human experience. Less than a philosophy of life, history, or civilization, science could never usurp the functions of art, ethics, religion, and politics.[25] As the most powerful human instrument, science needed to be integrated with the other great values of civilization.

Characteristics of Technology

In his analysis of technology in *The Social Foundations of Education*, Counts saw it as possessing six basic characteristics. Technology was rational, functional, organized, centripetal, dynamic, and efficient. The rationality of technology rested on its freedom from precedence. When given free reign, it destroyed traditional impediments to thought. It embraced a complex of immediately relevant ideas and methods that formulated and served human purposes. Containing its own criteria of authority and reflecting the scientific method, the use of technology required careful observation, inquiry, and accurate mathematical description. Quantitative reasoning, in turn, tested the outcomes of technology. By facilitating the ability to conjecture and predict outcomes, human freedom of action increased. As technology occupied ever-larger areas of the economy and as the engineering attitude developed, the inherent rationality of science would inevitably penetrate more deeply into social operations.[26] Functional rather than purely abstract, technology demonstrated its basically utilitarian nature when its findings were applied to the physical world.

Conceived and directed toward action, the use of technology required careful planning. Those who used and applied technology had to carefully formulate purposes, determine directions, and conceive plans of action prior to their actual undertaking. Operational plans had to be definite and based on positive knowledge of the ends to be realized. The method of

---

[25]Counts, *Education and American Civilization*, 257.
[26]Counts, *Social Foundations*, 70.

technology opposed impulsive and capricious individual actions. The age of technology required planning and coordination of economic processes, not the ruthless individualized competition enshrined in the doctrines of the classical economists.[27]

According to Counts, technology was centripetal in its nature. Dominated by rational design, it continually pushed into adjoining areas of the economy otherwise ruled by haphazard and chance operation. By drawing chaotic procedures within its ordered sphere, technology united and arranged adjacent operations around a common core of rational planning. It facilitated standardization in economic production and enhanced industrial consolidation. Legislative prohibitions on industrial consolidation were formal and ineffective. For example, the Sherman and the Clayton Antitrust Acts had failed to check the concentration of productive property into the hands of a small minority. Therefore, Americans had to be educated to recognize the centripetal nature of technology if they were to control industrial consolidation. This analysis, which stressed the rationality of technology, put Counts on the side of the advocates of a planned economy.

Counts claimed that technology was a dynamic force, since one invention or discovery stimulated a chain reaction of new inventions and discoveries. For example, the solution of a problem in physics or chemistry raised a second cluster of problems. The acceleration of change initiated by inventions and discoveries was not confined to the material realm, but quickly entered into cultural life and produced economic, political, moral, and social alterations. Technology's dynamic character vividly distinguished modern society from previous social orders.[28]

For Counts, efficiency was a pervasive characteristic of technology. Technological processes sought to achieve the greatest possible end with the least expenditure of energy and waste. Machine power made production efficient and extended the ideal of efficiency to human labor. From human labor, the spirit of

---

[27]Ibid., 71.
[28]Ibid., 72.

efficiency entered the entire community. Technology placed a premium on professional competence, since without the direction of the specialist's expert knowledge, the productive mechanism fell into chaos. As technology advanced, inexpert opinion yielded to trained intelligence.[29] Counts found technology's most striking characteristic to be its release of immense human power. In and of itself, technology, like science, was a neutral instrument. Its great power could serve noble and enriching ends or could be used as an instrument of selfishness and exploitation.

Finally, technology could not be viewed as a mere additive to American civilization. A culture, in Counts's opinion, was not merely an aggregation of discrete elements. It was rather a system of relationships that, in response to interior and exterior stresses and strains, continually altered patterns of life. Science and technology had unsettled both American and world cultures and had generated severe social and cultural dislocations. Both had produced a closely interdependent economy in which minute divisions of labor and the integration of many specialties necessitated national economic organization. Counts concluded that the individualistic economy conceived of in the days of the Manchester School of Classical Economic Thought was no longer in harmony with modern realities.[30] Adjustments were needed in economic institutions, social structures, education, government, religion, and morals, or civilization would collapse in disintegration and crisis.

In the economic realm, technology produced both specialization and integration as workers were subdivided into thousands of occupational specialties. This tendency toward differentiation and coordination contributed to technological efficiency. The simple handicraft production methods of an early American society dominated by occupational and social equality

---

[29]Ibid., 73.

[30]George S. Counts, "Presentday Reasons for Requiring a Longer Period of Pre-Service Preparation for Teachers," *National Education Association Proceedings* 73 (1935): 699.

were transformed into a vast, complicated, and costly machine process. The individual worker no longer owned the tools of production and the notion of occupational equality was shattered.[31]

Counts found occupational specialization closely related to the production of enormous quantities of goods for mass consumption, which in turn clearly enabled mass production. Otherwise, the vast productive capacity of the industrial complex would be purposeless. Unless the consuming masses could purchase the numerous commodities they manufactured, either a complete standstill or a greatly reduced level of operations would occur in a technologically organized industrial society. The Depression was caused by restricted purchasing power: mass-produced commodities exceeded the buying power of the consuming masses of the population.

Mass production had moved American civilization from a pain to a pleasure economy. Counts believed hunger and privation were unnecessary in twentieth-century America, since science and technology had created an extraordinarily powerful economic system. If the vast reservoir of potential economic power were rationally used, economic problems could be solved and poverty abolished.[32] In the pain economy based on scarcity, attempts to alter social patterns resulted in violence. In the abundant economy of technological society, violence was no longer needed to reconstruct society. By courageously and intelligently reconstructing economic institutions, man could obtain physical security and freedom.

Counts's published works emphasized the rise of technological society. His definition of technology in *Education and American Civilization*, 1952, was essentially the same as that given eighteen years earlier in *The Social Foundations of Education*, 1934. The most important and overarching task for Counts was to fashion a concept of democracy in harmony with industrial-

---

[31]Counts, *Education and the Promise*, 58.

[32]George S. Counts, "Theses on Freedom, Culture, Social Planning, and Leadership," *National Education Association Proceedings* 70 (1932): 250.

ized, technological society. On the basis of this, American educators could formulate a philosophy and program of education.

However, this step was blocked by an outmoded legacy of economic individualism. It is now proposed to examine Counts's criticism of economic individualism as an encumbering remnant.

Chapter 6

Economic Individualism and the American Experience

Despite a strong residue of economic individualism in the American outlook, technology demanded planning, cooperation, and coordination. Arguing that inherited doctrines of economic individualism confused and divided Americans, Counts believed their persistence aggravated the crisis as America moved from a pain to a pleasure economy. Counts's language during the Depression was part of the general preoccupation with economics as advocates of "private enterprise" jousted with proponents of a "planned economy."

While Counts's commentary on the contradictions generated by economic individualism reflected the climate of opinion of the Depression era, it held a significance that went beyond the turbulence of that troubled time. Counts's analysis reflected the social theory that was generated by other educational progressives such as John Dewey and William Heard Kilpatrick. Dewey's instrumentalism, expressed in *Democracy and Education*, 1916, exalted the educative role of the group and instructional methods based upon group problem solving. Counts shared the general Deweyan belief that the school was properly a social microcosm. Dewey's commentaries on social policy, *Individualism: Old and New*, 1929, and *Liberalism and Social Action*, 1935, stressed the theme that shared intelligence and cooperative action should replace the traditional American devotion to rugged individualism.[1] Counts shared the view that social policy should come from a popular and group-based consensus. His analysis was designed to demonstrate the inadequacies of economic individualism in a technological civilization.

The Origins of
Economic Individualism

According to Counts, economic individualism originated in an early period of American history, when North America's settlement coincided with the popularization of Enlightenment ideology. Rebelling against mercantilism, French physiocrats and British classical economists postulated a natural law of supply and demand, a concept of a self-regulating mechanism that worked to raise economic productivity. Claiming that government interference with this natural economic mechanism courted ruin and disaster, the classical economists established a rationale for private property, free enterprise, the profit motive, individual initiative, and unregulated competition.[2] According to a historical interpretation that saw the American Revolution as an economic struggle waged by colonial merchants against English mercantilism, economic individualism was an integral element in the struggle for American independence.

Counts traced the origins of economic individualism to early patterns of national settlement and development. North American settlement was primarily individualistic in that the transatlantic crossing and westward movement emancipated individuals from accustomed social controls. On the frontier, old class and community restraints were eroded as sturdy individualists fashioned their own instruments of government. After the long absence of legally constituted authorities, many fron-

---

[1] John Dewey, *Democracy and Education* (New York: MacMillan Co., 1916); *Individualism, Old and New* (New York: Minton, Balch and Co., 1930); *Liberalism and Social Action* (New York: G. P. Putnam's Sons, 1935).

[2] George S. Counts, *The Social Foundations of Education* (New York: Charles Scribner's Sons, 1934) 494.

tiersmen came to regard the state as a coercive and confining institution.[3]

Influenced by classical economic theory and the frontier tradition, the founders of the American republic viewed government as a negative force, as a passive regulator. Upon achieving independence, the framers of the American Constitution institutionalized these individualistic impulses into the fundamental law of the land. Revealing a deep distrust of strong government and collectivistic restraints, the Constitution separated governmental powers by a system of checks and balances.[4] When he devised a formula to deal with economic crisis, Counts argued that the system of checks and balances weakened government's capacity to respond quickly and effectively to urgent problems. The system also deflected and often blocked implementation of popular mandates.

Two Kinds of Individualism

During the Depression, Counts was among those who rejected the ideology of economic individualism. He contended that the advocates of economic individualism identified their favored economic theory with the democratic heritage to defer criticisms from economic planners. To expose this tactic, Counts examined the concept of economic individualism and found two types of individualism present in the American heritage. Widely different in origin, these two kinds of individualism varied in their social implications. The individualism of the independent freehold farmer of Jeffersonian democracy was far different from the individualism of the capitalistic entrepreneur bent on profit making in industrial society.[5] He believed that policymakers needed to differentiate between these two types of individualism.

---

[3]Ibid., 490.

[4]Ibid., 497.

[5]George S. Counts, "Presentday Reasons for Requiring a Longer Period of Pre-Service Preparation for Teachers," *National Education Association Proceedings* 73 (1935): 697.

America's exploration and settlement had generated individualism in the freehold farmer. Breaking numerous ties with the past and emancipating individuals from inherited social controls, frontier life also weakened the sense of community. Because of America's rich natural resources and sparse population, the freehold farm was an economic unit based on the nuclear family. Encouraged by the Pre-Emption Act of 1841 and the Homestead Act of 1862, the American economy came to rest on separate households and small towns dependent on the freehold agrarian economy.[6] However, Counts stated, the freehold farm was not an individualistic enterprise; it was actually based upon familism. On the freehold farm, solidarity existed as family members divided their labor and shared goods and services.

The rise of the entreprenuerial business classes created individualistic values that differed from those of freehold familism. Since it originated when feudalism was disintegrating, the middle class struggled for liberation from commercial restraints. Property-accumulating merchants and businessmen led the assaults upon the citadels of mercantilism. In a classic statement of Anglo-Saxon liberalism, John Locke's *Second Treatise on Government* limited government's functions to preserving property, maintaining freedom of contract, and providing for the free operation of economic forces.[7]

With the rapid industrialization after the Civil War, business and industry gained a dominant position in the United States. Although using slogans of economic individualism derived from the classical economists, American business leaders deliberately reduced competition. Eventually, private business silently repudiated laissez-faire doctrines and entered into commercial combinations to control the market price. With their emphasis on *caveat emptor*, business leaders were accused by Counts of often being indifferent to the general welfare. In responding to their actions, Counts condemned "the individualism of the few

---

[6]Counts, *Social Foundations*, 490.
[7]Ibid., 492.

which destroyed the individualism of the many, and made possible the aristocracy of today."[8]

Economic Individualism
in the 1930s

Although the American heritage contained two widely varying sources of individualism, a superficial theoretical fusion of the two had occurred. Counts claimed that slogans such as "individual opportunity," "rugged individualism," and "free enterprise" were used to counter arguments for a planned economy during the 1930s. In *The Prospects of American Democracy*, 1938, he warned against becoming enslaved by the glory of past victories. Although the concept of individualism was a great moral and political achievement of the American people, it became a liability when used merely as a mythic symbol.[9]

During the Depression Counts charged that privileged economic classes had distorted the conception of the individualistic American heritage. He identified the American Liberty League, which opposed President Roosevelt's New Deal legislation, as an organization of privilege. Although the Liberty League vociferously defended individualism, Counts charged that its members included those who had actively undermined the earlier individualistic economy and were attempting to foist the rule of property on the American people.[10] Representing concentrated wealth, the league practiced political deception by using a man of humble origins, Alfred E. Smith, as its spokesman.[11] Counts felt strongly that the ideology of economic individualism was incapable of preserving democracy in a technological era. By the 1930s gross inequalities in distribution of wealth, poverty, unemployment, slums, and privation among the great masses of people demonstrated the breakdown of the individualistic eco-

---

[8]George S. Counts, *The Prospects of American Democracy* (New York: John Day Co., 1938) 230.

[9]Ibid., 232.

[10]Counts, "Presentday Reasons," 696.

[11]Counts, *Prospects*, 234.

nomic order. He stated that this was evident in the financial collapse of 1929 when the anarchy of economic individualism brought the nation to the brink of ruin.[12]

Counts's rejection of the individualistic economy as a foundation of American democracy was not due to any inherent conflict between the freehold and business traditions of individualism. American democracy owed a debt to the developments wrought by individual owners of private property. Unfortunately, the close historical connection between the two individualistic traditions had produced a conception of the heritage that hampered the realization of democratic principles during the modern era.[13] Vested economic interests were manipulating historic ideological symbols to block needed reform.

Counts reasoned that technological forces, working since the industrial revolution, had eroded the foundations of the individualistic old order. American civilization had moved to the threshold of a new technological social order. Counts prophesied the demise of economic individualism when he stated:

> The familiar doctrine that the common good is best served if each individual is encouraged to pursue and safeguard his own interests will have to be rooted out of our mores and institutional life. This means that private capitalism with its dependence on the profit motive, the principle of competition, and private ownership of natural resources and the tools of production will either have to be abandoned altogether or so radically transformed as to lose its identity. In its place must come a highly socialized, coordinated, and planned economy devoted to the task of making science and the machine serve the masses of the people.[14]

---

[12]Counts, *Social Foundations*, 498.

[13]Counts, *Prospects*, 81.

[14]George S. Counts, "Secondary Education and the Social Problem," *School Executives Magazine* 51 (August 1932): 519.

Economic Collectivism

During the Depression Counts frequently claimed that the era of individualism had ended and that the frontiers of this collective age were opening. His editorial in *The Social Frontier* in November 1934 claimed that collectivism was a *fait accompli* since technology already had destroyed the individualistic economy and had created an economic interdependence.[15] The vast, complex, and interdependent economic mechanism, dependent on the preparedness and rationality of technology, demanded more coordination, direction, and control. Arguments for or against collectivism were superfluous since it was already a reality.

Rejecting unregulated capitalism based upon laissez-faire economic doctrines, Counts argued that the economic crisis of the Depression had accentuated the need for government intervention in the economy. When the Depression revealed the inability of business leaders to propose realistic solutions to the problem of economic crisis, leadership gravitated to the government agencies and economic theorists. Counts stated that the separation between politics and economics and between private and public interests had collapsed and that a sense of the common interest was emerging.[16] The individualistic ethic that promised progress through competition had failed. Arguing that competition was not only wasteful but also impossible in a technological age, Counts's address to the Progressive Education Association in April 1932 called for economic planning:

> Obviously, the growth of science and technology has reached a point where competition must be replaced by cooperation, the urge for profits by careful planning, and private capitalism by some form of socialized economy.[17]

Counts urged educators, especially progressives, to initiate reforms to educate the American people about the nature of the

---

[15] George S. Counts, "Collectivism and Collectivism," *The Social Frontier* 1 (November 1934): 3.

[16] Counts, *Social Foundations*, 504.

[17] George S. Counts, "Dare Progressive Education Be Progressive?," *Progressive Education* 9 (April 1932): 261.

emerging collectivist society. He regarded debates about the merits of the old individualistic order and the emergent order of collectivism as purely academic; for in order to frame a viable action program, Americans had to accept the reality of collectivism. Acceptance of a cooperative economy, he said, should come through realistic thinking and not as a result of external compulsion. It should be a free adaptation emerging from knowledge, thought, and understanding. Collectivism was not to be feared; the real menace to American liberty would come from a dictatorship of a powerful minority, or worse, the tyranny of ignorance and incompetence.[18]

Origins and Nature
of Collectivism

During the 1930s Counts, as an educational ideologist, was associated with a concept of collectivist society. His association with this concept derived from a variety of influences. For example, he was a member of an influential circle of progressive educators who shared a Deweyan belief in the educational potency of the human group. If cooperative learning were an effective means of bringing about educational progress, then shared associational inquiry also could be applied to social, political, and economic problems.

Counts was also familiar with and shared to some extent the cooperative impulses that emanated from such movements of American social reform as The Grange, farmers' alliances, Populism, and Progressivism. These movements looked to popular organization rather than to individualism for reform. Coincidentally—as already noted above—Counts was involved as a comparative educator with a study of Soviet society and education, a study that led to his eventual disenchantment with Soviet policies, although he remained impressed by the claims of Soviet planning and modernization.[19]

---

[18]Counts, *Social Foundations*, 529.

[19]Unpublished diary of George S. Counts's auto tour through the Soviet Union (1929) in George S. Counts Papers, Special Collections/Morris Library, Southern Illinois University at Carbondale.

In many respects, Counts and his intellectual and educational associates resembled a pale American version of the British Fabians, the intelligentsia associated with the Labour party. As noted previously, Counts was a supporter of trade and industrial unions, and an active leader in the American Federation of Teachers. He also was affiliated with third-party movements such as New York's Liberal party. These intellectuals, proponents in the 1930s of national planning and a cooperative society, lacked the influence that the Fabians had in Great Britain, since they never attained a leading voice in a major American political party.

An examination of Counts's concept of "democratic collectivism" requires recognition that a variety of influences had an impact on his thinking. The events that led to the articulation of the concept of "democratic collectivism" were associated with Counts's role as a member of the American Historical Association Commission on the Social Studies in the Schools. In the early 1930s the commission, which included such leading social scientists as Charles A. Beard, Avery Craven, A. C. Krey, Charles Merriam, Jesse Newlon, and others, developed a critique of American society that endorsed a collectivist social order. Counts served as the commission's director of research, and his book, *The Social Foundations of Education*, 1934, was one of its publications. The members of the commission, especially Counts and Beard, used the word "collectivism" to describe what they believed would be the trend to social and economic organization in the United States.[20]

During its work and in reaching its conclusions, the commission debated the use of "collectivism" to describe America's future course. President Hoover's Commission on Recent Social Trends had used the milder term "associational" to describe the emerging interdependent society. Krey, Beard, and Counts decided to use the stronger word "collectivist" after considering for a time the adoption of the word "associational."[21] The adoption

---

[20]Counts/Beard correspondence. Unpublished letters exchanged by George S. Counts and Charles A. Beard, in Counts's manuscripts.

[21]Interview with Counts by the author, 21 December 1962.

of "collectivist" proved unfortunate in light of its association with the Soviet system. Yet these American scholars wanted to expressly proclaim the end of an individualistic economy and the rise of a cooperative social order. Counts argued that only by recognizing the collective nature of industrial economy could the contradictions of contemporary society be resolved; only by making the interests of the masses dominant could the democratic tradition be preserved and fulfilled.[22]

Although Counts believed a choice between individualism and collectivism was no longer possible, he still believed it was possible to choose the kind of collectivism under which the American people would live. Writing as the editor of *The Social Frontier*, Counts stated that "the rise of a collectivist order" is "irrevocable." The question of "the form which collectivism" would take in the United States was still open, however.[23]

Counts contended that some form of collectivism applied to all political and social systems that operated in a technological society. It applied to the systems of Communism, socialism, and Fascism as well as to democracy. Counts, though, vigorously rejected antidemocratic, totalitarian forms of collectivism. He claimed that the choice was between two forms of collectivism: one democratic and the other dictatorial. The former was devoted to popular interests while the latter served special class interests.[24] Democracy's advocates faced the challenge of fashioning a cooperative economy in terms of the democratic ideal that served both the spiritual and material interests of individual men and women.

State ownership, control, and operation were not the only ways to socially direct the economy. Believing that operational responsibilities should be placed on the respective laboring, technical, and managerial personnel, Counts claimed that economic integration could be achieved through a consultative commis-

---

[22]Counts, *Social Foundations*, 531.

[23]Counts, "Collectivism and Collectivism," 4.

[24]George S. Counts, *Dare the School Build a New Social Order?* (New York: John Day Co., 1932) 49.

sion, composed of representatives from the several economic
sectors.[25]

Summation of Counts's
Critique of Individualism

Counts found that American individualism emerged from
two points of origin: one was derived from the frontier freehold
heritage, and the other from laissez-faire capitalism. The freehold frontier tradition was based on a form of rudimentary interdependence, exercised on a primary level by the family unit.
In contrast, capitalistic economic individualism centered on
profit making. Unfortunately, these origins of individualism
have been obscured and merged into a theoretical justification
for the status quo based on a version of individualistic capitalism. The defenders of the status quo expropriated the historic
forms associated with frontier familism to justify economic individualism. To rediscover the true meaning of American individualism, it was necessary to return to the origins of the
individualistic impulse and to separate logically these antago-
nistic sources. Although technology and industrial complexity
characterized modern society, it was possible to enlist the concept
of frontier familism in building a nationwide familism, a humanitarian community centered in the democratic ethos.

Freedom in a Collectivistic Age

During the 1930s the advocates of economic planning were
bitterly attacked by the devotees of economic individualism. *The
Social Frontier* stated in 1935 that the beneficiaries of inherited
economic institutions were loudest in praising freedom and de-
precating collectivism. The spokesmen for the United States
Chamber of Commerce, the American Liberty League, and the
American Bankers Association were advancing the argument
that collectivism would result in the curtailment of freedom. But
the editors of *The Social Frontier* demanded to know what def-

---

[25]Counts, *Prospects*, 96.

inition of freedom these spokesmen of economic individualism were offering to millions of people victimized by economic insecurity.[26]

In refuting the arguments of the advocates of economic individualism, Counts claimed that collective action would open new areas of freedom to humankind. The distinction between freedom and collectivism was false. Based on an individualistic conception of freedom devoid of social content and human significance, such distinctions harmfully widened the gap between human need and obsolete economic institutions. The creation of a genuinely free and democratic life depended on transferring control of the nation's natural resources to the masses of people engaged in intellectual and physical labor.

True freedom did not mean the absence of government control as alleged by the proponents of economic individualism. Rather than a negative throwing off of restraints, genuine freedom was based on cooperative effort for social achievement. Freedom—essentially a group effort—derived from the growth of culture and was released in the union, specialization, and integration of power. Counts stated, "Without power there can be only the freedom of quiescence, resignation, and death."[27] Based upon social science research, social planning would increase freedom by giving humankind control over its destiny.

Counts, in *The Social Frontier*, stated that the crucial issue was one of controlling the power of collective energy. Technology increased the freedom of those who controlled the sources of this energy, which prompted Counts to ask:

> Is the emerging collectivist economy to be managed primarily in the interests—material and cultural—of that small fraction of the population which by one means or another has gained title to most of the wealth of the country? Or is it to be managed openly and honestly in the interests of the great

---

[26]George S. Counts, "Freedom in a Collectivistic Society," *The Social Frontier* 1 (April 1935): 9.

[27]George S. Counts, "Theses on Freedom, Culture, Social Planning, and Leadership," *National Education Association Proceedings* 70 (1932): 250.

masses of the people who do the work of the nation and live by the services which they render society.[28]

Among the opponents of collectivism, according to Counts, were many sincere liberals who feared that the growth of power aggregates would weaken individual freedom. His editorials in *The Social Frontier* traced this attitude to the failure of proponents of collectivism to offer an adequate notion of modern liberalism. The advocates of economic planning had not defined adequately the broad human ends to be served in a new social order. Not only was collectivism necessary in a world of large-scale production, corporate control, and human interdependence, it was the only means of securing a free and democratic life. If productive resources were to be democratized, American society could have restored equality of opportunity and elimination of economic insecurity. When social utility replaced the profit incentive, American society would achieve the opening of rich, abundant, colorful, and significant outlets for human creativity.[29]

By abandoning economic individualism, the haunting specter of economic insecurity would be banished. Instead of rejecting the ideal of individual worth, a cooperative democracy would encourage personal growth and cultivation. Finding the rational and humane organization of the collectivistic economy completely compatible with a life of material security and spiritual abundance, Counts stated:

> If all of us could be assured of material security and abundance, we would be released from economic worries and our minds set free to grapple with really important questions of life—the intellectual, the moral, and the esthetic.[30]

Rise of the Economic Aristocracy

During the 1930s Counts feared that control of American life might fall into the hands of an economic elite or "economic ar-

---

[28]Counts, "Collectivism and Collectivism," 4.

[29]Counts, "Freedom in a Collectivistic Society," 10.

[30]Counts, "Dare Progressive Education Be Progressive?," 262.

istocracy." This minority, which controlled industrial technology for private profit, used an obsolete definition of democracy to justify its existence. What is more, the economic aristocracy monopolized the mass media to argue for economic individualism. Counts's attack upon this group was the most distinctive characteristic differentiating his work in the 1930s from his later thought. *The Prospects of American Democracy*, in particular, illustrated Counts's antagonism to vested economic interests.

Counts's definition of aristocracy resembled that of John Taylor, an old-line Jeffersonian. Citing Taylor's *An Inquiry into the Principle and Policy of the Government of the United States*, 1814, Counts stated that an aristocracy existed whenever and wherever power resided in the "hands of a minority."[31] The new aristocracy of wealth, or plutocracy, entrenched itself behind protective barriers of legal conceptions and established institutional arrangements. Counts then cited Berle and Means in *The Modern Corporation and Private Property*, 1932, to allege that 200 corporations controlled almost one-half, or 49.2 percent, of the corporate wealth of the nation. In 1930 these same corporations controlled 38 percent of the business wealth and 22 percent of the total national wealth.[32] This monopolization of the productive wealth of the nation by a minority provoked Counts to assert that the overwhelming majority of American people were in danger of losing any control over their economic destiny. Since control of public policy tends to accompany control of economic arrangements, the locus of power resided in the hands of a minority, or in the words of Taylor, "an aristocracy."

If the tendency to concentrate wealth continued unchecked, Counts feared that American society would stratify into rigid socioeconomic classes. Intermarriage and family arrangements tended to solidify this economic aristocracy and reduce social mobility. Counts predicted that if the trend toward stratification

---

[31]Counts, *Prospects*, 55.

[32]Ibid., 52. Adolph A. Berle and Gardiner C. Means, *The Modern Corporation and Private Property* (New York: Commerce Clearing House, 1932) 32.

were continuous, the cycle of democracy in American life would close and a new feudalism, based on industrial control instead of land, would occur. When the cycle of economic stratification was completed in America, he foresaw the emergence of class organization, consciousness, and conflict. The location of an economic aristocracy at the summit of the socioeconomic hierarchy would be accompanied by the stratification of farmers and laborers at the bottom of the socioeconomic pyramid. Unless these tendencies were arrested, Counts feared the outbreak of violent and bitter class warfare in America.[33]

Counts believed that genuine social and economic democracy was being undermined in the immediate post-Depression era. Although democratic institutions remained, they were becoming a facade for a bureaucracy that did not penetrate to the basic issues of social and economic life. Throughout the American historical experience, the general tendency was to increase popular control. Despite the gravitation of economic power to an elite, Counts believed in the power of the electorate. In *The Prospects of American Democracy,* he stated that the central problem was to restore democracy in a society dominated by an economic aristocracy. Counts alleged that American legal institutions had promoted the accumulation of property in the hands of the few. Traditionally, the United States Supreme Court's interpretation of the "due process" clause of the Fourteenth Amendment had favored property rights over human rights.[34] As the Supreme Court cast its weight against New Deal legislation, it again was protecting vested property interests. To bring about reform, Counts called upon the people to create a new social order in which the accumulation of property by an aristocracy would be impossible.

The marshaling of public opinion against an economic elite required an educational effort. While time remained, a climate of informed public opinion had to be created to offset the en-

---

[33]Counts, *Prospects*, 60-65.
[34]Ibid., 67-70.

trenched power of the economic aristocracy. If neglected for too long, the normal possibilities for change in the American political structure would dissipate. The economic aristocracy already had a propaganda advantage since they could buy the services of the media.

Although the procedural basis for popular political control still remained, the economic aristocrats could translate their economic power into political power by using their wealth to influence both public officials and the voters. By exerting economic pressures through their powerful lobbies in Washington and the state capitals, the monied group could influence legislators and government officials. It was possible for the modern economic elite to take real control of government, although the vestiges of popular rule remained. In pointing to the hostility President Franklin Roosevelt experienced with the business interests of the nation, Counts accused the economic aristocracy of unduly abusing Roosevelt.[35]

The Use of Propaganda

Counts, who believed that the mass media possessed an immense educative power, felt that this power had often been misused. By controlling the mass media, especially the press, the vested economic interests could organize and conduct national propaganda campaigns for their favored candidates, parties, and policies. Although such interests were unsuccessful in the presidential campaign of 1936, Counts pointed to the success of the media campaign in discrediting President Roosevelt's judicial program in 1937.[36] The actions of the press owners during the Depression were similar to their behavior in earlier periods of the nation's history. Counts alleged that every popular movement and every progressive leader from Jefferson to Roosevelt had been condemned as subversive and un-American by those who controlled the press.[37] The propaganda barrage confused the

---

[35]Ibid., 277.

[36]Ibid., 220.

[37]Ibid., 113.

American people and obstructed an educational program designed to enlighten them as to the reality of the problems that
they faced as a people. In his proposals for a program of action
to stimulate reform, Counts called for an institute of propaganda
analysis that could present an objective examination of the major
issues facing Americans.

Weaknesses of the Aristocracy

Despite its economic power, Counts believed the economic
elite was morally and spiritually weak, since it lacked the strong
foundations that had sustained the older European aristocracies
based on birth. Without the traditional ties of blood, sensibility,
and honor, the American economic aristocracy was an immature
social class that was largely composed of ordinary persons who
had only recently emerged from the common masses by acquiring
productive property.[38] According to Counts, the American economic aristocracy did not perform any genuine national social
service. Although once serving to pioneer technological inventions, it had become decadent and parasitical. Through reckless
exploitation, it had depleted the nation's natural resources and
polluted the environment. To increase profits, it impoverished
its workers. The Depression demonstrated its incapacity to maintain the economic system in continuous and full operation. Un-
mindful of an obligation to the nation, the vested interests had
revealed their incompetence.[39]

In one sense, economic elitism in the United States was certain to be a victim of its own philosophy. Extreme economic
individualism, assumed by its disciples to rest on natural laws,
required no special theoretical or philosophical formulation. Fur-
thermore, the economic aristocracy lacked the leadership to provide the integration, coordination, and planning needed to use
technological resources efficiently. Indeed, the casual nature of
economic individualism militated against the cooperative effort

---

[38]Ibid., 278.
[39]Ibid., 275-76.

needed to achieve an integrated democracy in a technological era.

Critique of Capitalism

During the Depression years Counts's editorials in *The Social Frontier* bristled with attacks on the economic aristocracy and the unregulated capitalist system. He urged teachers to join with American working men and women who were struggling to form large industrial unions. He condemned capitalists for maintaining a low wage level, resisting labor organization, producing inferior commodities, and hindering the technical modernization needed to increase production. He attacked the profit motive for causing scarcity, inefficient management, and technological stagnation.[40] In addressing the Progressive Education Association, Counts denounced unregulated capitalism as "cruel and inhuman."[41] The major defect of the capitalist system, he said, was its failure to provide people with the economic security needed for personal independence and dignity. Counts's critique revealed that he had no sympathy with the American capitalism of the 1930s. For the survival of political democracy, Counts stated,

> Historic capitalism, with its deification of the principle of selfishness, its reliance upon the forces of competition, its placing of property above human rights, and its exaltation of the profit motive, will either have to be displaced altogether, or so radically changed in form and spirit that its identity will be completely lost.[42]

Urging Americans to make historic choices, Counts observed that all nations were organized according to a set of specific values. The emergence of contradictory and irreconcilable forces inevitably would result in the domination of the one over the

[40]George S. Counts, "Teachers and the Class Struggle," *The Social Frontier* 2 (November 1935): 40.

[41]Counts, "Dare Progressive Education Be Progressive," 261.

[42]Ibid.

other. The people of the United States would have to make major economic, social, and political decisions. To ensure the ascendancy of popular democracy, an informed, determined, and united popular will was necessary.[43]

Counts advocated an equalitarian democracy. In a technological age, he believed that cooperative control and organization were the only viable foundations for a genuinely democratic social and political order. Since collectivism could also be used for totalitarian and aristocratic means, Counts advocated popular control of the means of production and the large aggregations of capital. Voicing its attitudes toward the problem of achieving democratic collectivism, *The Social Frontier* stated:

> It views the present concentration of wealth and power in the hands of the few, with its implications of class rule and domination, as an oppressive obstacle to the personal growth of American boys and girls and as a perpetual threat to the liberties of the masses of the people. To those who say that collectivism means regimentation, the answer is that collectivism is upon us and that the only hope for freedom lies in the direction of a democratic control over the material sources of the abundant life.[44]

Counts's attacks on economic elitism and aristocracy were a unique characteristic of his work during the 1930s and reflected the climate of opinion during the Depression years. His book, *The Prospects of American Democracy*, 1938, voiced the most pronounced ideological attack on the "economic aristocracy." In his post-Depression works, his tone changed. In *Education and American Civilization*, 1952, Counts still warned against the concentration of economic power and cautioned the American people about its deleterious effect on the future of political democracy in the United States;[45] however, the term "economic

---

[43]Counts, *Prospects*, 77-78.

[44]Counts, "Collectivism and Collectivism," 4.

[45]George S. Counts, *Education and American Civilization* (New York: Teachers College Press, Columbia University, Bureau of Publications, 1952) 191.

aristocracy" disappeared from his later works. Other phrases such as "economic royalists" and "barons of privilege" were commonly used during the Depression. Counts's phrase "economic aristocracy" similarly illuminated the temper of the times. The use of such jargon should not be summarily dismissed as merely indicating momentary discontent. For the period of the 1930s, this language revealed Counts's basic attitudes as he surveyed the course of American civilization.

From a perspective that transcends the immediate period of the Depression, Counts's analysis of American individualism had a broader meaning. Like Dewey and other social reformist educators, Counts opposed the meaning of individualism that had grown out of a Darwinist view of social evolution. "Survival of the Fittest" and rugged competition, for them, were obstacles to modernization in the popular interest. The social and educational circle to which Counts belonged harbored a nostalgia for the neighborliness of America's rural and small-town past. For Counts, the family farm and neighborhood was the historical basis upon which a sense and spirit of modern cooperation could arise.

Chapter 7

Counts's Program of Action

The Depression of the 1930s was a catalyst that moved Counts from a primarily educational to an ideological position. His *Dare the School Build a New Social Order?*, in 1932, had challenged educators to confront the problems of economic dislocation and unemployment and had urged them to join progressive forces in creating a new society.[1] Two years later, in 1934, Counts's *The Social Foundations of American Education*, influenced by Charles Beard's economic interpretation of history, urged organized education to promote "democratic collectivism" in the United States.[2] His most pronounced ideological statement appeared in 1938 in *The Prospects of American Democracy*, which outlined a program of action for the American people.[3]

Counts's movement from the empirical research and school-survey techniques of the scientific movement in education had begun earlier, but it was his response to the Depression of the 1930s that put him in the arena of political and social ideology. After the Depression, a dimension of Counts's career remained politically activist as well as academic and educational.

---

[1]George S. Counts, *Dare the School Build a New Social Order?* (New York: John Day Co., 1932).

[2]George S. Counts, *The Social Foundations of Education* (New York: Charles Scribner's Sons, 1934).

[3]George S. Counts, *The Prospects of American Democracy* (New York: John Day Co., 1938).

To examine Counts's ideological orientation, the following definition is stipulated for the term "ideologist." One, an ideologist uses historical interpretation to shape current policies. While such an interpretation of history may or may not be accurate by canons of historical scholarship, nonetheless it is used to explain contemporary conditions and to justify future programs. Two, the ideologist's view of the past is used to explain social change in a way that suggests general social, political, economic, and educational policies. Three, the ideologist is systematic, suggesting specific programs and their implementation. During the 1930s Counts fulfilled all three of these ideological phases or stages.

The historical interpretation that supported Counts's ideology saw American society experiencing a profound transition as it moved from an agricultural to an industrial-technological society. The current crisis of the Depression was symptomatic of the larger issue: the needed reconstruction of inherited social, political, economic, and educational institutions, processes, and values in light of an emergent technological society. In terms of general policy, Counts urged Americans to develop a synthesis of democracy and technology and to create an attitude and process of "democratic collectivism" as the foundation of the "new social order." Although his critics decried the absence of a specific program in Counts's work in the 1930s, he did, in *The Prospects of American Democracy*, 1938, suggest such a program. It was in this volume that Counts surveyed the assets and liabilities in the American cultural heritage in order to estimate the capacity of the American people to achieve a profound reconstruction of their society.

Assets of the American Heritage

Counts identified the major cultural assets that could contribute to the creation of a new social order. Among the salient features of the American cultural heritage, he found: (1) an absence of the residues of medieval institutions and attitudes; (2) an open, experimental, and democratic willingness to test beliefs and values in light of human experience; (3) a strong sense of community; (4) an aversion to totalitarianism; (5) the weaknesses of economic elitism; (6) abundant natural and technical resources; (7) a sense of international security; (8) a highly developed political sense; (9) a growing fund of precise and systematic knowledge.[4]

American opportunities for social mobility were far greater than those available in Europe. Unlike many European nations, the American republic did not develop an official state church or a hereditary military caste. American social institutions were not stratified according to a master-servant system of relationship. Because of the egalitarianism of frontier and farm, the majority of Americans were committed to the Jeffersonian-Jacksonian ideal of democracy. According to Counts, the American sense of equality and mobility contributed to the possibility for social reconstruction.

Among the assets of the American heritage were religious pluralism, constitutional guarantees of religious freedom, and the absence of a state church. In Europe, official state churches often worked in a conservative fashion to perpetuate the status quo. Counts believed that enforced religious conformity was a legacy of feudalism that had impeded reform in Europe. Because of religious pluralism and diversity, some churches in the United States had supported the common people and popular reform. Counts urged Americans to be vigilant in combating attempts to destroy the constitutional separation of church and state.[5]

Further, Counts was grateful that the United States did not have a military caste. Historically, military elites subverted democratic institutions. Guarding against this danger, the Constitution subordinated military to civil authority and gave the people the right to keep and bear arms; indeed, pioneer Americans had defended themselves by their own arms. The common man's ability to use the great equalizers of the Colt 45 and the squirrel rifle had contributed to the success of the westward

---

[4]Ibid., 252.
[5]Ibid., 256-57.

movement.[6] Writing in 1938, Counts commented that the technological development of warfare virtually had nullified the constitutional provision.[7] After World War II, Counts, decrying the ascendancy of the military in national life, commented that the emergence of the military-industrial complex warranted political intelligence to control it and make it responsive to the popular will.

A convinced democrat, Counts declared that the democratic heritage was the greatest single asset of the American people. He argued that the American state did not rest on absolutist or mystical concepts. When it served popular interests, the state's essential characteristics were to be reinforced. When the state blocked the popular will, it should and could be transformed. Counts found that the political experience of the American people with popular government had produced an elastic temperament that was essential to democratic procedures and experimental processes.[8]

Americans in their westward march had transformed wilderness into homesteads. In much the same way, agrarian America was transformed into an industrial society. As industrialism had altered economic life, Americans also needed to inaugurate institutional changes in government, family, and community. Because they did not fear change, but rather equated it with progress and betterment, the American outlook facilitated experimentation.

Clearly a believer in the concept of "progress" emanating from theories of the Enlightenment, Counts wanted organized education to serve as an instrument of national progress. Optimistic in his outlook, Counts consistently argued that human intelligence could direct technological forces to achieve progress for all.

Counts claimed that the American predilection to the empirical and experimental was much in evidence in the material

---

[6]Interview with Counts by the author, 21 December 1962.

[7]Counts, *Prospects*, 258.

[8]Ibid., 262.

dimension of American culture. He commented that the popularity of President Franklin Roosevelt's pragmatic public policy in the New Deal demonstrated the transference of experimental attitudes to economics and politics.

Located within the philosophical ranks of pragmatism, Counts believed that the experimental tendencies inherent in the American experience were manifested in John Dewey's instrumentalism. He claimed that the average American was a commonsense instrumentalist who rejected absolute systems of thought and was willing to experiment, judge by consequences, and compromise.[9] Along with his endorsement of the scientific method, Counts also emphasized the creative role of the human group, as did Dewey. Counts believed that many Americans valued the neighborhood sense of community that was admirably suited to building a cooperative social order. Relying on Beard's view of history, Counts found the cooperative spirit operative in the American past. According to Beard, rugged individualism was tempered by the family, a spirit of cooperation, mutual helpfulness, and a sense of community. Such common frontier cooperative endeavors as barn-raising and threshing had curbed the egocentrism of rugged individualism. In their westward movement, pioneer settlers had formed groups for mutual protection against hostile Indians and a threatening environment.

Counts believed that the cooperative tendency derived from the American past would be of inestimable value in building a cooperative society. The predilection of Americans to participate in numerous civic, fraternal, and interest groups demonstrated the continuing vitality of "good neighborship." For Counts, the central task was to apply the principle of "good neighborship" to modern, urban, technological civilization.

As a man of democratic spirit, Counts rejected the totalitarian Communist, Fascist, and Nazi movements. He believed that the tactics of these dictatorships should convince Americans that the substitution of violence for democratic processes exacted a heavy and intolerable price. The example of the twentieth-cen-

---

[9]Ibid., 265.

tury totalitarians demonstrated that the separation of means from ends was inimical to democracy. The choice of incompatible means destroyed the ends proclaimed by revolutions spawned from the dictatorships of both extreme political Right and Left. Although both Communists and Fascists inscribed "freedom" on their banners, they fixed the yoke of tyranny on their victims. Undemocratic procedures formed undemocratic attitudes, which in turn supported the indefinite continuation of dictatorship. Neither Communism nor Fascism provided alternatives for Americans, liberal or conservative, to follow.[10]

During the Depression and afterward, Counts proclaimed that the abundant natural and technical resources of the United States were a great asset. If these resources were used rationally, it would be possible to solve economic problems and to create economic security, comfort, and even luxury for the entire population. Counts concluded that America's bountiful natural environment contained the resources needed to build a progressive and enduring civilization in an industrial age.

When he wrote in the 1930s, Counts believed that the geographical location of the United States protected it from external attack. Indeed, the Atlantic and Pacific oceans separated the United States from the major sources of European and Asian aggression. Although improvements in transportation had reduced their breadth, the ocean barriers were still sufficient to protect the United States from any sudden and unprovoked attack.[11] Despite this tendency to a "fortress-America" attitude, Counts had traveled widely and considered his foreign ventures among the most educative of his career.[12] When *The Prospects of American Democracy* was published in 1938, advances in military technology had not yet reached the point of directly threatening America's security. Nor did Counts wish to abandon the European democracies to Nazi totalitarianism. When the Nazi

---

[10]Ibid., 271-73.

[11]Ibid., 282.

[12]Interview with Counts by the author, 21 December 1962.

war machine began to sweep over Europe, he urged positive resistance on the part of the democracies.

Counts also believed that concerted efforts to avoid war protected American civil liberties. During the Civil War and World War I, wartime conditions had worked to limit civil liberties. During the Cold War of the 1950s, McCarthyism and antisubversive investigations had restricted intellectual as well as civil freedoms.

Believing that Americans could use gradual, peaceful, evolutionary means to solve the economic problems of the Depression, Counts generally supported New Deal legislation. He believed that a high cultural level, formal education, and actual living under democratic institutions had produced political literacy and understanding among the great majority of Americans.

For Counts, the presidential election of 1936 illustrated the good political sense of the American people. In this campaign, he said, reactionary elements used every conceivable demagogic device to discredit the Roosevelt administration. Concerted press and radio campaigns accused Roosevelt of seeking to destroy American democracy, using Fascist and Communist tactics, and attempting to enslave both business and labor. Despite this campaign of vilification, Roosevelt was overwhelmingly reelected to a second term as president. Counts credited the American people with a high level of political sense and civic competence in their resistance to political propaganda.[13]

Counts's support of the New Deal was based on choosing the most agreeable political alternative. He, like other progressive intellectuals and educators, criticized the New Deal for being overly tentative and a piecemeal rather than comprehensive approach to national reconstruction. Nevertheless, the New Deal was a much more agreeable political choice for Counts than the alternatives offered by Hoover, Landon, and the Republican party.

---

[13]Counts, *Prospects*, 285.

Counts saw the growing body of precise knowledge on human affairs as an element of great worth in reconstructing the American heritage. This knowledge had accumulated rapidly as scientists and researchers perfected their instruments of investigation. The American temperament, in particular, favored the growth of the social sciences. Unfortunately, this vast network of information was only a potential possession of the ordinary citizen. Educators needed to translate this theoretical knowledge into functional knowledge to equip Americans to deal intelligently with the problems of the age.[14]

Liabilities in the American Heritage

Counts's list of American assets was an optimistic catalogue of resources that could be marshaled to create a new social order. Unfortunately, he found these assets were offset, and often negated, by certain national weaknesses. He found the following liabilities present in the American cultural heritage: a concentration of economic power; the complexity of industrial society; a legacy of economic individualism; the heterogeneity of the population; the existence of outdated symbols and loyalties; a spread of spectacles and circuses; the rise of chronic unemployment; a long tradition of violence and intolerance; the system of checks and balances; and the failure of organized civic education.[15]

Foremost among the weaknesses Counts identified in the American cultural heritage were the concentration of economic power, the complexity of industrial society, and the legacy of economic individualism. Since the analysis of these weaknesses was so important in Counts's social theory, they have been examined in earlier chapters. These interrelated areas of weakness were significant obstacles to the reconstruction of American democracy along popular and cooperative lines.

---

[14]Ibid., 287-88.

[15]Ibid., 217.

For Counts, the heterogeneity of the American population was a potential obstacle to national reconstruction because sectional, racial, ethnic, and religious differences as well as varying social and political philosophies divided Americans into often-conflicting interest groups. These diversities were further exacerbated by historic conflicts between urban and rural interests.[16] Counts, like Dewey and other progressive educational theorists, believed that the prospects of American social and political renewal depended on the creation of a community of shared interests. Although Counts did not develop a methodology for unifying conflicting interests other than relying on democratic processes, he realized the need to unite Americans behind a philosophy and program of cultural reconstruction. Counts never advocated a culturally monolithic society, but he did fear that socially reactionary forces could manipulate special-interest groups to block cultural reconstruction.

While the democratic impulse in the American heritage could inspire cultural reconstruction, Counts stated that mere reliance on the symbols of the heritage could be limiting. Even as Counts continually emphasized the importance of civic education, he advised that an unenlightened chauvinism could foster extreme and irrational nationalism. Under the impetus of an irrational patriotism, some Americans believed that the United States enjoyed a special providential dispensation. Conceiving American civilization as superior to all others, super patriots believed American institutions were destined to be diffused throughout the world.[17] Chauvinistic irrationalism encouraged campaigns of "one hundred per cent Americanism" that distrusted all foreign ideas. Militating against needed reform, unthinking super patriots often smeared opponents as atheists, Communists, and un-American. Such an attitude, fired by prejudice, was a liability inherent in the American cultural heritage.

Counts referred to the "spread of spectacles and circuses" as an impediment to social reconstruction. Although his exact

---

[16]Ibid., 228.

[17]George S. Counts, *The American Road to Culture* (New York: John Day Co., 1930) 107.

meaning of "spectacles and circuses" was unclear, his phrase apparently described conditions during the decline of the Roman Empire when Romans flocked to the coliseum to witness entertainments sponsored by the ruling elites. According to popular history, the ruling elites blunted the discontent of the Roman masses by titillating them with lavish spectacles. Using the phrase to describe Americans' lavish attention to motion pictures and spectator athletic events, Counts believed modern "spectacles and circuses" diverted popular attention from serious social and political problems. The danger was that this concentration on trivialities rendered a large body of voters socially illiterate, politically indifferent, and unfit to rule.[18]

According to Counts, chronic unemployment and economic maladjustment were dangerous threats to the maintenance of democratic institutions. Economic instability produced feelings of helplessness, which in turn generated a social and political climate that was conducive to totalitarianism. Through the promise of jobs, potential dictators recruited followers from the disaffected among the unemployed. Counts believed that democracy was in peril as long as the economic crisis was unresolved.

Counts's study of American history convinced him that a strong tendency to intolerance and violence still existed in the American character. This propensity to violence, which developed on the frontier where firearms preceded law courts, was rooted deeply in American culture. During the Depression, Counts was alarmed by resorts to violence that surfaced in disputes between organized labor and capital. He feared that reliance on violence impeded peaceful negotiation and adjudication of labor-related disputes. Counts, who sympathized with organized labor, feared that the concentrated economic power of capital would triumph in any armed encounter. Further, the "economic elite" had the advantage of influencing the formal police power of the state and the propaganda power of the media.[19]

---

[18]Counts, *Prospects*, 236.

[19]Ibid., 237-44.

Like other experimentalist-inclined progressive educators, Counts strongly believed it possible to apply the scientific method to resolve social and political problems. His arguments for a rationally planned society were evidence of this process-oriented method. In addition to theorizing, there was also an ideological and activist inclination present in Counts. His rhetoric during the Depression contained overtones of class struggle, but at heart he clearly preferred peaceful processes.

Counts, who was active in the movement for civil liberties, condemned the tradition of intolerance in American life. From the time of the "Know-Nothings," nativism in America had blocked progressive social reform. Racial, religious, and ethnic discrimination had been used as a wedge to divide those who otherwise shared genuine economic interests. Believing that the democratic ethic rested on a foundation of equality, Counts strongly objected to racial, religious, social, and ethnic discrimination.

Charging that government had not responded energetically enough to the Depression, Counts discerned that certain structural weaknesses impeded governmental action, particularly at the federal level. The highly dynamic character of technological society, which increased the role of the federal government, made hesitancy and delay costly and dangerous. Government's hesitancy to cope with the crisis of the Depression was an example of an outmoded belief in the role of limited political institutions. In Counts's mind, the American system of checks and balances often thwarted the popular will. Bureaucratic and legal apparatuses often reversed popular decisions and enabled the vested economic interests to rule politically in spite of the will of the electorate. As an illustration, Counts cited President Roosevelt's difficulties in enacting the New Deal legislative program. Elected by an overwhelming majority in 1936, Roosevelt sought to use political institutions to secure economic reforms. The vested economic interests had used their vast power to influence the mass media and legislators against the president's program and had succeeded in paralyzing the government's ability to combat the Depression. Counts regarded the system of checks and balances and the separation of powers as a serious impediment to using democratic processes for fundamental economic and social reforms.[20]

As an educator, Counts criticized organized education for its failure to prepare Americans to deal with the technological age. His criticism of educational traditionalism and its policy of ideological neutrality was voiced dramatically in *Dare the School Build a New Social Order?*. He continually urged educators to become educational statesmen who would deliberately lead in bringing about needed social reconstruction rather than blindly follow the patterns of the past.

Counts thus examined the assets and liabilities inherent in the American cultural heritage. The assets could be used to build a new social order and construct a viable concept of American civilization in the industrial age. Only the future would determine whether the assets outweighed the liabilities. Counts believed that if the full energies of the American people were committed to reconstruction of the heritage, the effort would triumph.

After discussing the strengths and weaknesses of the American cultural heritage, Counts developed a plan of action. Some working hypotheses were needed to guide the American people if they were to recreate a conception of democracy suited to the needs of a technological society. Following the instrumentalist approach, the means and ends of the program were to be shaped by experimental processes.

Basic Purposes of
the Plan of Action

Counts wanted his analysis of American civilization to be the basis for a "civilization philosophy" of education that would stimulate political discussion and the dissemination of social knowledge. As part of his program of action, he sought to develop a conception of civic education that was committed to social planning and reconstruction. However, the urgency of the Depression demanded immediate and vigorous action as well as

---

[20]Ibid., 246-47.

philosophical reformulation. Counts urged Americans to act before the vested interests of modern feudalism, the economic aristocracy, destroyed the possibilities of democratic experimentation.

Counts knew that creating a concept of democracy for a technological age would be a formidable challenge that required popular intelligence, experimentation, and innovation. If violent revolution occurred before the social intelligence of citizens was adequate to resolve the crisis, the nation might fall prey to dictatorship. The crisis demanded a comprehensive program of organized education to meet the challenge and to avoid a possible drift into dictatorship. Although recognizing that the preservation of American democracy was a race between immediate education and catastrophe, Counts also realized that orderly social reconstruction could not proceed more rapidly than the advancing experience of the American people. Therefore, a philosophy and program of education to meet the needs of a democracy in a technological age were a vital part of Counts's program of action.

Since the urgent problems of the Depression were economic, Counts outlined several general proposals for economic reconstruction: (1) the American heritage was to be dissociated from its historical connections with the old individualistic economy; (2) the interdependent economy was to be recognized as an economic reality; (3) the economic system was to be organized and administered for the common good.

Generally, Counts modeled his new economic order on a notion of democratic collectivism. Referring to extant public-service programs, he argued that the collective approach had a tradition in the United States. Mails, highways, schools, water supply, and sewage disposal were areas for which government had long ago assumed responsibility. In the future, Counts asserted that the community must intervene to conserve and develop the basic natural resources of land, timber, water, and minerals necessary to the public welfare and formerly exploited by private interests. He further called for the socialization of services tending toward monopolies, such as communications, transportation, energy, and banking. To achieve such community intervention and control, a large measure of coordination and economic planning was necessary.

Counts also urged adoption of measures to curb the powers of economic privilege. The masses of people were encouraged to organize both as consumers and producers, in cooperatives, labor unions, guilds, and granges. Gift and inheritance taxes were recommended until the great fortunes had been gradually reduced. Counts was advocating a mixed economy, with both public and private sectors coexisting and cooperating. While public-service areas such as communications, transportation, energy, and banking would be in the public sector, other businesses would operate in the private sector. However, alongside of these private businesses, there would also be a range of cooperatives.

A New Leadership

The organization and administration of the complex technological economy—a delicate and complicated mechanism—required a new, highly trained and specialized leadership whose preparation presented a challenge of great magnitude to organized education. The education of the new leaders was fundamental in any program of action; for Counts regarded the older concept of leadership originating in simpler societies as insufficient to the modern era. The Depression had revealed the incapacity of both traditional political and business leaders. Not due to a native lack of talent among American people, this incapacity reflected the inadequacy of traditional methods of identifying and choosing leaders, which separated political from economic leadership. Although older methods had functioned well in agrarian society, they were unsuited to a technological society of political and economic integration.

According to Counts, leadership in a technological society would come from the various functional groups composing society. Instead of amateur politicians, the new leadership required energetic, capable, and highly trained persons who were advanced in the fields of their specific knowledge and expertise. Eventually the most capable would reach the highest positions of leadership. Counts stated:

The function of leadership will then be to lead rather than to follow. Genuine leadership involves a certain measure of moral or intellectual ascendancy over the masses which is traceable to some real superiority. While the highest type of leadership neither bamboozles nor coerces, it also never truckles or flatters. It leads because it can challenge, inspire and point the way. Such leadership is required today in every department of life.[21]

Counts's comments on future leadership predicted the emergence of a corps of experts, which would be a consequence of social organization according to economic function. Although he never specified the exact form for political organization of this future society, his estimate of the coming leadership pointed to some pattern of corporate state. However, whatever exact political form the new leadership took, it had to be committed to the democratic heritage. Inherent in the emergence of such a leadership was the danger of separating leaders from the masses of people. Counts attempted to minimize this danger by committing both the masses and leaders to a similar conception of the American heritage produced by a commonly shared education.

A Program of Action

After generally considering the broad outlines of the new society and its leadership, Counts developed a nine-point program of action: (1) a commitment to the values and efficacy of democratic processes; (2) dissemination of knowledge necessary for free people; (3) comprehensive popular organization; (4) effective popular organization; (5) maintenance of a complete monopoly of military police power by legally constituted authorities; (6) the guaranteeing of civil liberties; (7) the systematic exposure of political propaganda; (8) conservation of the democratic temper; and (9) avoidance of war.[22] Such a program,

---

[21]George S. Counts, "Theses on Freedom, Culture, Social Planning, and Leadership," *National Education Association Proceedings* 70 (1932): 251.

[22]Counts, *Prospects*, 353.

Counts believed, would serve as a guiding policy for long-range social reconstruction.

The Democratic Process

A vital element in the American historical experience, the democratic heritage provided the necessary inspiration to meet future challenges. For Counts, faith in political democracy was a necessary foundation for the programs of action. He believed that if Americans lacked the democratic faith, their will to use orderly processes to adjudicate differences would be blunted. Loyalty to democratic processes would ensure that the general welfare was put above selfish, special, or factional interests.

Knowledge for Free People

Counts believed the dissemination of knowledge was necessary for free people to understand and solve social problems. The democratic processes required intelligent decision making. For knowledge to be used effectively, it had to be organized and made available to the masses of the population. The effectiveness of political action in a democratic society required free and full discussion of major issues and problems. For Counts, any program calling for the dissemination of knowledge involved the creation of a systematic program of education, from childhood through the adult years, to prepare people to make intelligent policy decisions. The success of the program of action prescribed by Counts depended upon a system of organized education that was capable of providing the skills and knowledge required for lucid decision making in a democratic society.

Comprehensive Popular Organization

Counts did not believe that the problems facing American civilization could be solved by the genius of a single individual. On the contrary, a functioning democracy in an era of technology required the comprehensive organization of the people, so that they could promote their own education and form policies to defend their interests and liberties. Counts reasoned that the democratic elements of the population had to "unite their forces and secure concerted action" to avoid dispersing their efforts.[23]

In a modern, industrial society, Counts found the most effective lines of organization were based on production. Revealing his deep sympathy for the labor-union movement, Counts termed the organizations of manual workers the "democratic clubs of the present day, defenders of popular rights, foes of aristocracy, and the most powerful bulwark against the resurgence of autocracy."[24] Because of mass production's tendency to separate workers from the tools of production, the individual worker could gain security only through association and combination with his fellow workers.

Counts found the movement toward industrial unionization advancing rapidly due to the policies of the Roosevelt administration. He urged continuing worker organization until it encompassed the great majority of the laboring and farming population and embraced the clerical, technical, and professional people as well. Counts put his theory of labor organization into practice, especially by his activity in the American Federation of Teachers, of which he was president from 1939 to 1941.

Counts believed that consumer cooperatives were another useful form of popular organization. While the effectiveness of consumer cooperatives in dislodging the power of the vested interests was still uncertain, Counts felt that these cooperatives pointed the way to a cooperative society. Urging popular organization on the broadest possible basis, Counts asked opponents of the rule of privilege to unite in using technology for the common welfare.

He warned advocates of cooperative popular organization to guard against the machinations of special privilege. Vested special interests, using the Machiavellian principle of "divide and conquer" to destroy the unity of the common people, raised false issues to confuse the ranks of organized labor. They further exploited cleavages in the ranks of common people by dividing

---

[23]Ibid., 179-81.

[24]Ibid., 182.

farmers from urban dwellers and the manual from the white-collar workers. Cautioning the common people not to be misled by such diversionary tactics, Counts warned that only popular comprehensive organization would advance democracy in a technological age.

Effective Popular Mandates

For peaceful political solutions to remain feasible in meeting the problems of the age, government had to execute popular mandates quickly, efficiently, and honestly. If government temporized, it would become impotent during crisis and eventually lose popular respect. In commenting on government's response to the Depression, Counts commended President Roosevelt for his energy and courage in meeting the economic and political crisis. However, as the Depression receded, powerful vested interests levied a campaign of abuse and misrepresentation against the president that undermined his program despite Roosevelt's overwhelming mandate in the election of 1936.[25]

Finding the Supreme Court an obstacle to the execution of popular wishes, Counts alleged that the Court had a record nullifying legislation aimed at controlling corporate wealth and power. By protecting the concentration of property, the Court blocked the popular will.[26] Undoubtedly, a good deal of Counts's antagonism toward the Court derived from its striking down legislation such as that providing for the National Industrial Recovery Act.

Counts argued that any program of action required the government's effective execution of popular mandates. Because of the social crisis and increased burdens placed on public agencies by the complexity of technological society, local and state governments lacked the capacity to effect needed solutions to the major problems of the age. Of necessity, such problems were the concern of the national government, which Counts believed had to operate in these areas until some kind of decentralization

[25]Ibid., 187-88.
[26]Ibid., 191-92.

emerged based upon the functional divisions inherent in the closely integrated society of the future.[27]

Monopoly of Military Power

The success of any program of action required that the legally constituted government maintain a monopoly of military and police power. Freedom was safe only where military and police power were subjected to legal discipline. Although the founding fathers realized the importance of keeping military power in the hands of the people, the Second Amendment to the Constitution guaranteeing "the right of the people to keep and bear arms" had been rendered null by the rapid technological advances in military armaments. The machine gun and the tank had rendered the frontiersman's long rifle pitifully obsolete. If military and police power gravitated out of the control of the legally constituted government and into the hands of private interests, most of the population would be powerless to resist the coercion of armed force.

In the 1930s Counts detected a tendency for the diversion of military and police power from legally constituted authority into the hands of the vested interests. Demonstrating his pronounced sympathy with organized labor, Counts stated that the employers' use of strikebreakers threatened government authority.[28] In Europe during the 1930s, private armies and "free corps" had subverted legally constituted government. Storm troops in Germany and Fascist legionnaires in Italy had destroyed political opposition and rendered legal authority impotent. Lessons of this sort could not go unheeded in the United States.

Counts continued to devote serious attention to the problems of military force. In his lectures in Brazil in 1958, Counts stated that citizens of a free land must anxiously view the brute facts of power lest some class, caste, sect, or party monopolize military, economic, or political power. The power inherent in the new weapons of warfare constituted a grave threat for the future of

---

[27]Ibid., 190.

[28]Ibid., 194.

liberty.[29] Counts also reflected his concern about the growing military power in *Education and the Foundations of Human Freedom*, 1962.[30]

Civil Liberties

The peaceful reconstruction of society required the maintenance of the guarantees for basic civil rights. For Counts, the great liberties written into the national and state constitutions such as freedom of speech, belief, press, assembly, and petition constituted the essence of the democratic process. He found that business interests were the most flagrant violators of civil liberties. A terrifying record of abuse of civil liberties existed in the capitalist policies of strikebreaking and labor spying. In any program of action, the heritage of civil liberties must be protected as an unassailable principle of democratic life.[31] As a means of voicing these convictions, Counts was a member of the American Civil Liberties Union and served on its National Committee.

Exposure of Propaganda

Counts's program of action required the concerted efforts of the great mass of the American people. Only through the diffusion of pertinent and vital information could great decisions be made and policies formulated. He pointed to the attempts made by vested interests to manipulate the mass media in order to divide the common people. To defeat the attempts to influence people through propaganda, a massive study and exposure of political propaganda was needed. The press, radio, and motion pictures required the constant scrutiny of an informed public. Although a liberal press might accomplish this task, the estab-

---

[29]George S. Counts, *Educacao para uma sociedade de homens livres na era technologica* (Rio de Janeiro: Centro Brasileiro de Pesquisas educacionais, 1958)

[30]George S. Counts, *Education and the Foundations of Human Freedom* (Pittsburgh: University of Pittsburgh Press, 1962).

[31]Counts, *Prospects*, 197-99.

lishment of a completely independent institute of propaganda analysis appeared the most promising solution. Charged with examining personalities, organizations, and interests, the institute would appraise the newspapers, periodicals, motion pictures, and other media on the basis of truthfulness, balance, fairness, and general integrity. Schools, colleges, churches, civic organizations, and groups of farmers, laborers, and professional workers would be kept informed of the information dispensed by the propaganda analysts.[32] By the systematic exposure of media propaganda, the air could be cleared of confusion and the common people could be better prepared to decide major issues.

Conservation of Democratic Temper

Counts called for the conservation of the democratic temper, since the orderly functioning of political democracy required a commitment to certain procedural methods. Recognizing the communal interests served by democracy, all parties had to agree to operate within the framework of democratic processes. Adherence to a democratic temper demanded a willingness to accept the verdicts of election, place the general welfare above private interests, refrain from mob violence, get to the facts, and compromise. For Counts, the democratic temper was a necessary unifying element in a society marked by diversity and conflict.

Avoidance of War

Arguing that the preservation of the democratic way of life required a peaceful world, Counts considered the problem of American foreign relations. The warlike posturing by the European dictators in the late 1930s deeply troubled Counts, who maintained a keen interest in foreign affairs. As mentioned previously, he was a serious student of Russian society and education and had traveled widely. Because of his own personal experiences, he did not isolate the United States from the world community. Although emphasizing America's unique cultural

---

[32]Ibid., 203.

experience, he saw the United States as part of an interdependent world.

Listed as the final point of his program of action in *The Prospects of American Democracy*, war was to be avoided if at all possible. An especially long and severe war might lead to the overthrow of domestic democratic institutions and promote dictatorship. He cited his close friend and associate, Charles A . Beard, who had pointed out that the wars of 1812, 1861, and 1917 had all fortified the power and rule of special interests over the needs of common people.[33] In light of the delicate condition of American democracy during the 1930s, war could prove fatal to the democratic heritage.

Innovations in military technology during the modern era made war especially frightful. Counts stressed that man had achieved a degree of control over natural forces that made him capable of destroying the human race.[34] Despite the awesomeness of war weapons, contradictions existed in world affairs that could easily bring humanity to the brink of disaster.

In *The Social Foundations of Education*, 1934, Counts's treatment of the contradictions in world relations was essentially economic. The earth and its resources were apportioned among nations claiming to be fully independent and sovereign. Along with the dangers of unrestricted sovereignty, the internal economy of every capitalistic nation contained elements that induced conditions conducive to war. According to Counts, capitalism required an "ever-growing market for manufactured goods" and an unsatiated appetite for raw materials. One consequence of economic competition was a "struggle for markets and raw materials" that drew nations into the struggle. Counts wrote that war is "financially profitable" to private munitions makers. Thus in every country "mighty forces, usually economic in character, are tending to disrupt the peace."[35]

---

[33]Ibid., 204.

[34]Unpublished MS. (n.d.) by George S. Counts, "The Meaning of a Liberal Education in Industrial Society," 7.

[35]Counts, *Social Foundations*, 526.

Counts's ascribing the cause of war to economic factors was reinforced by the tendency of many historians to attribute World War I to economic rivalries. The investigation of the Nye Committee of the United States Senate convinced many Americans that the First World War resulted from the machinations of money lenders and munitions makers. Although enjoying popularity during the 1930s, this view oversimplified the realities of international affairs. In 1941 Counts corrected the earlier view in *The Social Foundations of Education.* He stated that in 1934 his mind was so completely directed to property relationships that he had minimized the question of military force. He further acknowledged that the rise of the Communist and Fascist dictatorships in Europe demonstrated that the power of the machine gun was far more decisive than the power of property.[36] Military technology used to support such dictatorships negated the possibility of carrying out successful revolution against such regimes.

When in 1938 he urged the avoidance of war as part of the program of action to preserve democracy, Counts found that the United States was experiencing a serious dilemma in foreign policy. If the United States assumed a responsibility for defending democracy abroad, it might destroy freedom at home. On the other hand, if the United States attempted to isolate itself completely, it might become the ultimate victim of Fascism; indeed, maintaining a strict policy of neutrality might actually aid aggressor nations. Lacking a definite policy framed in the interests of the American people, the United States might conceivably be made the instrument for advancing the exclusive and vested interests of her own economic aristocracy or the ruling class of some foreign nation.

To avoid war, Counts identified what he considered to be the four realities of international relations. One, the distribution of the earth's population bore little relationship to the distribution of natural resources. The nation-state system of the past was

---

[36]Counts, "A Liberal Looks at Life," *Frontiers of Democracy* (May 1941):232.

out of harmony with the realities in the balance of forces and interests. Two, the extreme nationalism of Germany, Italy, and Japan had served notice on the world community that they would not respect the formal principles of treaties or international law. Three, technological advance had produced worldwide interdependence. Four, the inherited institutions and arrangements, domestically and internationally, manifested a high degree of instability.[37]

In view of these international realities, Counts proposed a nine-point foreign policy designed to block our conscious or unconscious involvement in international conflict. One, the United States, recognizing the distinction in moral position between nations in conflict, should use its diplomatic power to aid the victim of aggression. Two, an economic embargo should be placed on aggressor nations. Three, the United States should permit its citizens to aid the victim of aggression in every possible way. Four, the United States should withdraw its forces from the areas of aggression and conflict; all risks involved in residence or participation were to be borne by the private citizen and not by the nation. Five, the United States should refuse to be drawn into war by international incidents. Six, the domestic economy should be strong enough to bear any ensuing dislocations. Seven, the national military defense should be so formidable that any attack from without would be impossible. Eight, a program of international cooperation should be undertaken to remove the injustices in natural-resource distribution. Nine, the American people should devote their energies to creating a state of social justice in which no political opportunist would seek to escape domestic problems through foreign adventures.[38]

Counts's views on foreign relations that appeared in *The Prospects of American Democracy*, 1938, reflected a post-World War I perspective. The proposed policies represented the view that a strongly defended America would be an impregnable fortress. In all fairness to Counts, it should be pointed out that as

---

[37]Counts, *Prospects*, 210-12.
[38]Ibid., 212-13.

of 1938, the nature of Nazi and Japanese aggression had still not been fully understood by most observers. Although still primarily concerned with domestic policy in 1938, Counts began to turn more of his attention to America's role in foreign affairs.

Course of Action Summarized

In his earlier discussion of American society during the 1930s, Counts traced most of the immediate crisis to economic problems based on the legacy of economic individualism and the rise of economic elitism. Outside of urging wide popular organization, the bulk of Counts's program was designed to educate the mass of people in order to more efficiently execute the popular will through political action. His analysis of the origins of American democracy implied that political institutions and processes were a product of economic conditions. Counts's program of action also suggested that it was possible to reverse the economic pattern through concerted political and educational activity. His program of education and political action was designed to check the tendency to economic and social stratification occasioned by the economic crisis.

The program elucidated by Counts was a relatively moderate approach to the problems of the 1930s. Even as economic depression had jeopardized political action, Counts sought a political and educational solution to the problem. Instead of violence or radical change, he urged a program of experimentation to secure needed reform. Foremost in the entire program of analysis and action, should be the formulation of a deliberate program of education committed to securing economic, social, and political change and preserving the American democracy. The acceptance of this course of action could lead to a long-range program of reconstruction that would integrate the American democratic ethic with the realities of the emergent technological society. With this needed adjustment, American civilization consciously could chart its course through the transition from an agricultural to a predominately industrial way of life.

If a viable educational philosophy and program were to be formulated, a clear and consistent conception of American civilization was necessary. A philosophy of education that took the problems of American civilization into view could be expected to produce informed citizens with the capability of meeting the challenges of the emerging new social order. Counts's analysis of American civilization inevitably led to a formulation of an educational philosophy and program directed to achieve that end. It is now appropriate to begin a discussion of Counts's educational theories and policies.

Chapter 8

Counts's Civilizational
Philosophy of Education

George S. Counts was best known as an American educational theorist. He began his career in professional education as a person who skillfully combined statistical analysis with sociological theory. He gradually moved to larger social issues and to the study of the historical origins of these issues. At various times in his long career, Counts was noteworthy as a professor of education at Columbia University's Teachers College, as a student of Soviet society and education, as a leader of the American Federation of Teachers, and as a force in the Progressive Educational Association. In preceding chapters, Counts's concept of American civilization has been examined. Chapter eight will survey his "civilizational philosophy" of education.

In some respects, Counts's educational philosophy resembled John Dewey's instrumentalism in that it was experimentally based. However, in other important aspects, it differed from Dewey's philosophy. Dewey's orientation was primarily process-oriented in that he saw education as resulting from the use of the scientific method to solve problems. While Counts valued the experimental method, he also emphasized the cultural context in which the method of science was to operate. Indeed, Counts's interpretation of the American heritage, his exaltation of a particular conception of democracy, and his emphasis on technology all provided a framework for the operation of the experimental method.

Counts's analysis of American society produced both a theory of social change and an educational philosophy designed to meet the needs of American democracy in a technological era. His approach to educational theory was basically relativistic in that education was a function of a particular civilization at a particular historical period. Counts's philosophy for American education was rooted in the democratic heritage and in the dynamics of an emergent technological society.[1]

Counts's educational philosophy was based on his interpretation of social change and on the interpretations of American historians and social scientists. His relativistic interpretation saw social and cultural development as particular to the earth's climatic and geographical regions. Education, both as a general process of enculturation and as a particular process of schooling, was conditioned by the needs of individual societies. Unlike educational theorists such as Robert Hutchins or Mortimer Adler, who viewed education in universal terms, Counts emphasized it as culturally relative and, he hoped, culturally relevant. American education and American schools were part of a unique civilization that had its own problems, potentialities, and resources. For Counts, political, social, cultural, and economic institutions, processes, and problems determined the course of American education. The democratic tradition of the United States was to be reflected in its educational philosophy. Since human history was the record of changing social, political, and economic relationships, educational policies also varied within a given historical period.

Rejecting any universal concept of education, Counts viewed it from the orientation of a culturally based pragmatist. In *Dare the School Build a New Social Order?*, he said that those who conceived of education as eternal truths or in universal terms isolated schooling from political, social, and economic realities.[2]

---

[1]Counts's educational relativism is examined in Gerald L. Gutek, *The Educational Theory of George S. Counts* (Columbus: Ohio State University Press, 1970) 3-15.

[2]George S. Counts, *Dare the School Build a New Social Order?* (New York: John Day Co., 1932) 17-18.

Rather than being confined to a devitalizing set of abstractions that were remote from life, education should respond to changing human needs, problems, and purposes. Again, American education needed a program that responded both to its democratic tradition and also to the emergent reality of an industrialized, technological, and mass society.[3]

With his emphasis on the varying social and institutional patterns characteristic of different societies, Counts stressed the intimate relationship between group life and education. His early book, *The Principles of Education*, 1924, stressed the educational significance of the group. Born into the group, human beings learned the knowledge and skills that perpetuated and regenerated the society. Through group association, human experience was transferred from one individual to the entire society. Group association was also the means of connecting individuals with their past. Shared knowledge, through common symbolic and linguistic patterns, became a cultural inheritance that was transmitted from generation to generation and thus perpetuated the cultural life of the society.[4] For Counts, education deliberately sought to introduce the young to the knowledge, skills, and values of their particular civilization.[5]

While education preserved the cultural inheritance of the group, Counts believed that this preservation was selective. As his analysis of the American heritage shows, he believed that traditional cultural residues that impeded social reconstruction ought to be rejected and discarded. For example, the legacy of economic individualism and *laissez-faire* philosophy was to be abandoned deliberately in order to facilitate social planning and engineering.

---

[3]George S. Counts, *The Prospects of American Democracy* (New York: John Day Co., 1938) 357.

[4]J. Chapman Crosby and George S. Counts, *Principles of Education* (Chicago: Houghton Mifflin Co., 1924) 23-24.

[5]John L. Childs, *American Pragmatism and Education* (New York: Henry Holt and Co., 1956) 241.

The School in Society

Like John Dewey, Counts saw education as a means of bringing the immature person into group life by providing experience
with the use of cultural instruments. Since all human association
was educative, learning occurred not only in the school, but took
place wherever and whenever individuals interacted with their
social group.[6] However, the school, as society's formal educative
environment, was consciously established to facilitate the introduction of the young to their culture.[7] The school was an agency
through which students acquired the perspective to evaluate and
judge events.

In Counts's view, the American school was not to be isolated,
but was to be closely related to other social institutions. As a
social agency functioning in an increasingly interdependent and
technological civilization, the school was related to the economic,
political, and cultural institutions of the society. Nor could
knowledge be treated in isolation from social purposes. The
knowledge transmitted by the school should be a cultural instrument for solving social problems. If these issues involved
social or political controversy, the school should not ignore or
evade them, but should seek to solve them. Nor could the school
refrain from making value judgments. Since the school introduced the young to their society, it was inevitably concerned
with values. The value pattern prescribed by the school reflected
the cultural heritage of the particular society. Worthwhile education, therefore, required an examination of the historical and
contemporary culture to find the values appropriate to that
civilization.

During a time of profound cultural transition such as that
which American civilization was experiencing, educators had to
choose between conflicting value patterns as the United States
moved from an agrarian-individualistic to a technological-co-
operative social order. In fulfilling its normative role, the school

---

[6]George S. Counts, "The Place of the School in the Social Order," *National
Education Association Proceedings* 64 (1926): 310.

[7]Chapman and Counts, *Principles*, 46-47.

faced two alternatives: (1) imposing conflicting values; (2) choosing between conflicting values. Counts urged educators to make a statesmanlike choice between these conflicting values. Since the emergent social order required the inculcation of cooperative values, American schools ought to undertake the needed value education.

Due to the acceleration of social change, the school needed to perform functions that had been done in preindustrial society by other agencies. Counts urged educators to examine consciously how the functions of other institutions had been transformed by social and technological change. Believing that organized education should contribute to social planning and direct change, Counts urged greater freedom for educators to develop policies to promote social welfare. The formulation of educational policies would be difficult in the crucial and controversial areas of economics, politics, morals, and religion, where opinion was divided.

Theoretical Reconstruction in Education

In *The Principles of Education*, Counts argued that every age needed its own restatement of educational philosophy. Rapidity of social change, advance of human thought, and changing conceptions of human psychology rendered any final formulation of educational philosophy impossible. As society changed, educational aims, values, and purposes evolved; educational objectives and methods required reconstruction to meet the needs of changing times.[8] Occupying a strategic location, education was at the very heart of the process of cultural reconstruction.[9] To cope with the myriad problems of cultural transition, Counts urged the formulation of an educational philosophy adequate to social demands. Reflecting great historic choices, the formulation of an educational philosophy would embrace analysis, selection, and synthesis. It involved making choices among possibilities, the selection and affirmation of values, and the framing of policies.

------

[8]Ibid., 81.

[9]Unpublished MS (n.d.) of George S. Counts, "The Meaning of a Liberal Education in Industrial Society," 2.

These decisions were conditioned by the requirements of time and situation. Education could not occur in a transcendental vacuum that was devoid of historical and social reality. Both the social sciences and psychology would be useful tools in formulating a realistic educational philosophy.[10]

In the past, educators had neglected social and cultural problems and had confined their activities to superficial and mechanical solutions. They had failed to deal with the central task of educational theory—the problem of relating education to American civilization.[11] In restating the task, Counts argued that a great conception of education could proceed only from a bold and creative confrontation with the traditions, conditions, and potentialities of civilization.[12] In dealing with the problems of technological change and modernization, Counts's charge to educators was a sweeping one:

> In transforming the plane of social living from insecurity to security, from chaos to planning, from the private profit audit to that of collective utility, from the lurid contrast of vulgar !uxury and dire want to the shared abundant life made possible by technological advance, an organized educational profession can play an important role. Whether society will master and control technology for the good of the masses of the population, or whether the present forms of social living separating the bulk of mankind from ownership, control, and the full benefits of a power civilization lingering in their ever increasing decrepitude, depends among other things on the degree to which organized education actually identified itself with social reconstructive forces.[13]

---

[10]Counts, *Prospects*, 318.

[11]George S. Counts, *Education and the Promise of America* (New York: Macmillan Co., 1946) 20.

[12]George S. Counts, *Education and American Civilization* (New York: Teachers College, Columbia University, Bureau of Publications, 1952) 399-412.

[13]George S. Counts, "Educating for Tomorrow," *The Social Frontier* 1 (October 1934): 5.

Counts urged educators to reconstruct a concept of American civilization and to formulate a philosophy of education that would help to build a society that enriched the lives of the common people by affirming the democratic impulse. For him, the central task of American educators was to apply the ideas, values, and processes of democracy to a technological society.

Education and American Social Policy

As indicated, Counts regarded education as an important instrument of social and political philosophy. Profound social change had occurred as the United States moved from the old, agrarian, rural neighborhood into a society that was highly complex, industrialized, scientific, and technological. From a loose aggregation of relatively self-contained households, the nation— under industrial impetus—had become a vast society characterized by minute structural and functional differentiation.[14] While rapid change was most evident in the material dimension, social, moral, political, economic, religious, and aesthetic patterns were also being transformed. The crisis of American civilization was produced by the society's unpreparedness to deal with and direct the processes of social change. American educators had failed to equip the nation's citizens with the outlook and methodologies needed to solve the problems of social change. Severe social crisis and disintegration occurred because of man's inability to reconstruct his environment rationally and efficiently.[15] For Counts, a cultural lag had developed as human practical inventiveness surpassed social organization and ethical consciousness.

To Counts, the crucial educational task was that of formulating a philosophy of education that would face the problems of social change and that would contribute to the reconstruction of ideas, beliefs, and values in light of an emergent technological society. A twofold task faced American educators: (1) creating

---

[14]George S. Counts, "Orientation," *The Social Frontier* 1 (October 1934): 3.

[15]Counts, "Meaning of a Liberal Education," 1.

an educational philosophy that came from the American democratic heritage; (2) using this philosophy in an open-ended way to develop an experimental temperament that would stimulate Americans to solve the problems of acute cultural crisis and potential social disintegration.

Since he viewed education as relative to a given society, Counts saw organized education in the United States as the product of a particularly American heritage. In *The Social Foundations of Education*, Counts expressed his relativistic orientation when he argued that education was "always a function of time, place, and circumstances."[16]

A viable educational philosophy for American civilization in the twentieth century had to affirm the values embodied in the historic American democratic tradition and recognize the dominant contemporary reality: the emergence of a technological civilization. Using these two postulates, American educators would create educational and social policies that would attempt a fundamental national reconstruction. The broad aims of such an educational policy would be that of harnessing the powers of science and technology to realize democratic goals, to preserve personal integrity in a matrix of organized and cooperative activities, and to achieve efficient and popular control of an intricate and complex social and economic mechanism. The creation of a comprehensive philosophy of education encompassed the entire range of human activities. Economics, politics, international relations, aesthetics, recreation, literature, family life, and the mass media all had to be considered in formulating an educational philosophy.[17]

An educator who integrated all of the above elements of American life into his policies would truly be an educational statesman. Counts reserved this term for that minority of educators willing to recast educational goals in line with the civi-

---

[16]George S. Counts, *The Social Foundations of Education* (New York: Charles Scribner's Sons, 1934) 1.

[17]George S. Counts, "Dare Progressive Education Be Progressive?," *Progressive Education* 9 (April 1932): 262.

lization's changing demands. Insensitive to the need for moral leadership, American educators had long concentrated on their own specialties, or on mechanics, or on administrative arrangements, thereby neglecting the major social and economic problems facing American society.[18]

Counts promoted work in educational reform as one of the highest forms of statesmanship available to Americans. Counts hoped that the American educator—in rising to his role as an educational statesman—would foster the maximal development of citizens, upon whom the state depends for existence, security, and fulfillment. The educational statesmen Counts envisioned would assume responsibility for formulating educational goals and policies rather than acceding to the dictates of powerful special-interest groups. Statesmanship involved, above all, the courage to make historic choices based upon the cultural heritage, technological change, and present social trends.[19]

Counts dismissed in advance any philosophy of education that would disregard the influence of the democratic ethic and modern technology. In arriving at the compact term, "democratic ethic," Counts had spent considerable time identifying the major tendencies of the American democratic heritage. It is worthwhile to reassemble these tendencies here in sequence. First, the uniquely American concept of democracy had exalted all of the following in its brief history: the freehold, the frontier, and the face-to-face, popular democracy of Jefferson and Jackson; the progressivism of Wilson, the liberalism of Roosevelt; and the attempts of a planning society as expressed in the New Freedom, the New Deal, the experimentalism of John Dewey, and the historical relativism of Charles Beard. In emphasizing the progressive-liberal strand of the American tradition, Counts automatically rejected the conservatism of Hamiltonianism, Social Darwinism, economic individualism, and unregulated capitalism.

---

[18]Unpublished MS (n.d.) of George S. Counts, "Proposed Study of Education and Culture in an American Industrial Community," 10.

[19]Counts, *Social Foundations*, 4-5.

Second, American democracy was not only a political expression; it was and should continue to be a product of the economic, social, moral, and aesthetic forces operating within the culture. Third, equality was indelibly located at the roots of democracy, since only in a society of equals could democracy flourish. Any action—whether social, economic, or political in nature—to subvert the egalitarian foundations of American democracy should elicit vigorous opposition from democracy's proponents.

Educational leaders would also have to relate the democratic heritage to the emergence of an industrialized and urbanized society that was a product of the modernizing forces of science and technology. Counts saw technology as a cultural force as well as a material one. Since technology exhibited characteristics that were rational, functional, centripetal, dynamic, and efficient, the new education should also cultivate the same qualities and attitudes in the citizens who would inhabit the Republic and hopefully chart the course of American society.

Counts's examination of the American cultural heritage affirmed two essential strains: an equalitarian, democratic ethic and the emergence of a scientific-industrial-technological society. These two tendencies were to be the basis of a reconstructive synthesis that constituted the framework for a civilizational philosophy of American education. Although it ought to embrace both democracy and technology, Counts did not want an educational philosophy that was deterministic or that limited human intelligence in shaping its own future. Relying on the open-endedness of instrumentalism, Counts wrote that America's future depended on the ability of its citizens

> to learn from experience, to define the problem, to formulate a program of action, to discover, appraise, and marshall the apparent and latent, the actual and potential resources of American democracy.[20]

Although he believed that the school had been a potent force in shaping American culture, Counts did not exaggerate the

---

[20]Counts, *Prospects*, 350-51.

school's power. He felt that Americans had tended to overemphasize the power of organized education. Because of what amounted to an immature faith in organized education, Americans often regarded the school as being capable of solving all problems. This uncritical American faith in the school tended to inhibit serious inquiries into education's social and ethical foundations. Although many Americans viewed the school as a democratic agency, history demonstrated that a popular form of organized education existed for particular polities.[21] The totalitarians of the twentieth century proved adept at using organized education as an ideological instrument to advance their political programs.

Counts believed that the exaggerated claim of the school's power was not only a popular misconception, but was frequently shared by professional educators as well. Some educators, including many identified with progressive education, erroneously thought that the school was an omniscient agency capable of reconstructing society without the intervention of social institutions. By neglecting the educative role of other social institutions such as the family, the media, and the community, these educators had isolated the school from its cultural context. Educators, if they were to be effective, had to maintain a constant awareness of social change. An educational philosophy that was based solely on events that occurred within the school was doomed to be devitalized and unrealistic in its programs.[22]

In the 1960s and 1970s, educational theorists, especially historians and sociologists, began to direct attention to distinctions between education and schooling. In particular, Bernard Bailyn and Lawrence Cremin were identified with the thesis that the school was but one of many educational institutions and that much education occurred outside of the school.[23] Counts's *The*

---

[21]George S. Counts, "Education for What?," *The New Republic* 71 (May 1935): 22.

[22]George S. Counts, *The American Road to Culture* (New York: John Day Co., 1930) 18.

[23]Bernard Bailyn, *Education in the Forming of American Society* (New York: W. W. Norton and Co., 1972) and Lawrence A. Cremin, *Public Education* (New York: Basic Books, 1976).

American Road to Culture in 1930 clearly anticipated the distinctions between education and schooling that became prominent in educational circles some thirty years later. While his comments on education as a general process and schooling as an institutionalized setting for education were often blurred, Counts recognized that a wide range of institutions and agencies exercise an educative function in society.

When he asked educators to "Build a New Social Order," Counts urged them to join with those progressive social forces that exemplified modern democracy. He did not intend for educators to attempt a single-handed social reconstruction. As educational statesmen, they could provide leadership in creating a new society. Although the school's power to reconstruct society was indeed limited, Counts felt that organized education should do more than merely reflect the traditional attitudes and values of the status quo. Counts opposed a merely reflective theory because this meant that powerful interests could easily dominate organized education.

A democratic program of education, Counts believed, would cultivate democratic habits and commitments and would provide the knowledge needed for intelligent participation in political and economic life. In acting as a democratic community, the American school should strive to develop a sense of personal competence and adequacy in those who attended it. It should cultivate allegiance to human equality and brotherhood, and emphasize the democratic processes of discussion, criticism, and decision making. Its orientation should be both democratic and scientific.

As his analysis of the American heritage revealed, Counts was partial to a particular interpretation of the democratic tradition. Although every civilization produced its own conception of education, he did not treat these versions of culture and education with impartiality. He was biased and committed to the democratic ethic within a technological culture. The primary obligation of American educators was to clarify the underlying assumptions that gave purpose, structure, and procedures to the school.

As each new generation of Americans was introduced to its cultural heritage, it acquired knowledge, skills, and values. Without the possibility for cultural transmission, American democracy would perish. The release of creative human energy occurred, not by isolating a person from tradition, but by identifying him with a vital and growing tradition through which he could find self-realization. Tradition was not to be thought of in static terms, but rather as a process of humanization that was ever changing and evolving. Counts stated:

> The real question, therefore, is not whether some tradition will be imposed by intent or circumstances upon the coming generation (we may rest assured that this will be done), but rather what particular tradition will be imposed. To refuse to face the task of selection or the refashioning of this tradition is to evade the most crucial, difficult, and important educational responsibility.[24]

In urging educators to commit themselves to the fostering of democratic and technological values, Counts was challenging two widely divergent groups of educational theorists: the traditionalists and the child-centered progressives. The traditionalists conceived of education as being purely cerebral and unrelated—at least in the immediate school context—to social and political issues. For traditionalists, education was to cultivate a detached and objective intellectuality. They feared that if the school became involved in controversial issues that had an immediate economic, political, or social relevance, then instruction would become a program of indoctrination for a particular point of view. As already indicated, Counts regarded this orientation as either an unrealistic avoidance of crucial issues or an apology for the status quo.

It should be pointed out, however, that Counts was a firm believer in the importance of both organized subject matter and problem solving. Education, for him, was not an either/or affair.

---

[24]George S. Counts, "Theses on Freedom, Culture, and Social Planning and Leadership," *National Education Association Proceedings* 70:249.

He believed that to solve problems as an adult, one had to have experience in dealing with problematic situations as a child. For this reason, Counts also quarreled with the child-centered progressive educators who insisted on complete freedom. He attacked their support of a completely neutral school environment in which children were never imposed upon, but were completely free to develop according to their own interests and needs. Only as a member of society who participated directly in his culture could the child grow through experience. As a cultural sharer and participant, the child was imposed upon by the culture, but was also an agent in transforming that culture.

Counts's position as an educational theorist was a clearly articulated one. He believed, as we have noted, that education was always relative to a given cultural context. It transmitted a cultural heritage to the immature members of the society. But the inculcation of a cultural heritage was not a simple matter of handing over the whole past to a child. Rather, it was an ethical matter of selecting parts of the cultural heritage.

For Counts, the school was not an isolated social agency but instead part of a complicated web of institutions. Educators, if they were to lead society rather than follow the dominant interest groups, needed to base their educational programs on a knowledge of social and technological change. In other words, Counts argued for a philosophy of education that was committed to preserving and extending the democratic ethic in a society that was technological in character.

Chapter 9

The Impact of Counts's Analysis of Soviet Education on His Theory of American Civilization

George S. Counts was prominent not only as a leading analyst of American education, but also as a pioneer in the study of Soviet culture and education. Counts's interest in Soviet education grew out of his appointment as associate director of Teachers College International Institute in 1927. In his autobiographical sketch, Counts wrote that each member of the institute was expected to develop expertise in the language, schools, and basic institutions of a foreign country. Counts elected to study the Soviet Union, which he visited in 1927, 1929, and 1936. After Lenin and his Bolsheviks came to power, Counts wrote that he was

> challenged by the proclaimed goals of the Soviet government to extend educational opportunities to all, to eradicate racial and national prejudices and hatreds, to prevent depressions, and to bring the economy, science, and technology into the service of the people.[1]

---

[1]George S. Counts, "A Humble Autobiography," in Robert J. Havighurst, ed., *Leaders in American Education: The Seventieth Yearbook of the National Society for the Study of Education* (Chicago: University of Chicago Press, 1971) 161.

In the early 1930s Counts was impressed by what appeared to him to be the extensive and popular planning that was taking place in the Soviet Union's First Five Year Plan. However, he stated that he had "grave doubts and misgivings about" the Soviet dictatorship. Despite his hopes that the evils of dictatorship "would weaken and disappear," the "exact contrary happened" as the Soviet dictatorship "became ever more ruthless" and totalitarian.[2]

While the thrust of this book is intended to examine Counts's theory of American civilization, a brief examination of his views of Soviet culture and education is useful in illuminating the evolution of his thought. Counts was a prolific author of articles and books on the Soviet Union, its culture, and educational system. Particularly revealing of his first impressions of Soviet life, culture, and education is Counts's diary of his 6,000-mile automobile tour of the Soviet Union in 1929.[3] He conducted a series of interviews with Soviet officials and educators who were charged with popularizing and implementing the First Five Year Plan. M. M. Piotrak of the Department of Social Education told Counts of that department's efforts to draw great masses of people into the planning process and to develop a collective work psychology. Counts was told consistently in these interviews that Soviet planning was popularly based, extensive, and had enlisted the entire range of informal educational agencies, such as motion pictures, the press, and art, as well as the formal educational agency of the school. As the Great Depression deepened, Counts called repeatedly for popular and centralized planning to end the economic crisis. He never suggested emulation of the Soviet model, but believed that the United States needed planning and concerted collective effort to create a society free of economic want and scarcity.

Counts's first book on the Soviet Union, based on impressions of his automobile tour, was *A Ford Crosses Soviet Russia*, a

---

[2]Ibid.

[3]George S. Counts, "Diary of 1929 Automobile Tour in the Soviet Union," in George S. Counts Papers, Special Collections/Morris Library, Southern Illinois University at Carbondale.

descriptive and anecdotal account published in 1930. This was followed by his more systematic academic study, *The Soviet Challenge to America*, in 1931. In 1943 he and John Childs wrote *America, Russia and the Communist Party in the Postwar World*. The year 1947 saw the publication of *I Want to Be Like Stalin*, written with Nucia Lodge, which was a translation of a Soviet pedagogical text. By 1949 Counts had become a severe critic of Soviet mind control, which he condemned in *The Country of the Blind*, also written with Nucia Lodge. His most comprehensive and mature treatment of Soviet education was *The Challenge of Soviet Education* in 1957.[4]

In the span of twenty-seven years from 1930 to 1957, Counts's views of the Soviet Union underwent a profound transformation. It should be indicated that in many respects Counts's changing interpretations of the Soviet Union were part of the changing milieu of Soviet-American relationships. Over more than four decades of studying the Soviet Union, Counts changed from a friendly and curious visitor, to a scholar impressed by Soviet planning and modernization, to a critic who saw the Soviet regime as a powerful and sinister threat to human freedom. This fluctuation in Counts's attitude toward the Soviet Union paralleled the shifting opinions of many other mainstream American liberals. It is revealing to note that his two major books on the Soviet Union have the word "challenge" in their titles: *The Soviet Challenge to America* (1931) and *The Challenge of Soviet Education* (1957). The challenge that Counts described was based on the Soviet attitude, conditioned by Marxism-Leninism, that history's inevitable course involved a coming clash between the Communist and the capitalist nations. In 1931 the Soviets

---

[4]Counts's major works dealing with Soviet culture and education are: *A Ford Crosses Soviet Russia* (Boston: Stratford Co., 1930); *The Soviet Challenge to America* (New York: John Day Co., 1931); with John Childs, *America, Russia and the Communist Party in the Postwar World* (New York: John Day Co., 1943); with Nucia Lodge, *I Want to Be Like Stalin* (New York: John Day Co., 1947); with Nucia Lodge, *The Country of the Blind* (Boston: Houghton-Mifflin Co., 1949); *The Challenge of Soviet Education* (New York: McGraw-Hill Book Co., 1957); *Krushchev and the Central Committee Speak on Education* (Pittsburgh: University of Pittsburgh Press, 1959).

defined the challenge to be the task of overtaking and surpassing the industrial and technological development of the capitalist countries, particularly the United States. By 1957 Counts interpreted the challenge to be a worldwide threat by the Soviet Union to human freedom and democratic institutions.

Counts's *Soviet Challenge to America*, in 1931, was written against the background of the Great Depression of the 1930s. Like many other liberal intellectuals and pragmatic-progressive educators, Counts had endorsed social planning as a means of solving the national economic crisis. His works on American education during the 1930s such as "Dare Progressive Education Be Progressive?," *Dare the School Build a New Social Order?*, *The Social Foundations of Education*, and *The Prospects of American Democracy* identified the absence of social planning as a major cause of social and economic crisis and urged that American government, society, and education embark on a program and process of comprehensive social planning.[5]

Counts saw the Soviet Union as a nation that had committed itself deliberately to thoroughgoing social planning for the purpose of modernizing a large but backward nation.

Counts's foreword to *The Soviet Challenge* shows that the economic crisis was on his mind as he contrasted the American failure to plan its way out of the Depression with the Soviet Union's massive experiment in comprehensive national planning. He wrote that the Depression "has turned the minds of economists and statesmen . . . to the question of social planning." He charged that America's "present economic, educational, and political leadership has thus failed to rise to the opportunity created by science and technology."[6] After criticizing the Western and American inability to establish planning mechanisms and procedures, Counts then turned to his subject and wrote:

---

[5]George S. Counts, "Dare Progressive Education Be Progressive?," *Progressive Education* 9 (April 1932): 257-63; *The Social Foundations of Education* (New York: Charles Scribner's Sons, 1934); *The Prospects of American Democracy* (New York: John Day Co., 1938).

[6]Counts, *The Soviet Challenge to America*, ix.

The world today is full of social experimentation. There is one experiment, however, that dwarfs all others—so bold indeed in its ideals and its programs that few can contemplate it without emotion. Because of the clouds of passion which still envelop it, there is serious danger that its most revolutionary, though less sensational, features may escape adequate notice. Soviet Russia is endeavoring with all the resources at her command to bring the economic order under a measure of rational control. She may fail in the attempt, but in the meantime every student of human affairs should follow the effort with breathless interest. She issues to the Western nations and particularly to the United States a challenge—perhaps one of the greatest challenges of history. But she issues not through the Communist International, nor through the Red Army, nor through the Gay-Pay-OO (political police), as most of our citizens naively and timorously believe, but through the State Planning Commission and her system of public education.[7]

When Counts first wrote these words, the Soviet Union was in the midst of its First Five Year Plan, which had been launched in 1929. Counts identified the central aims of the plan as being: (1) the rapid industrialization of the Soviet Union and (2) the radical socialistic reconstruction of village life. The Soviet planning process, as he saw it, was involved in widespread popular discussion as ideas flowed back and forth through the various groups, unions, and agencies of the country. The planning process involved two major groups: one, specialists and technicians such as economists, engineers, educators, and planning experts who developed the economic, technical, and scientific components of the plan; two, party members, government officials, and representatives of the masses who scrutinized the plan from political, ideological, and practical perspectives. Finally, the State Planning Commission developed a general plan, in which the various commissariats for agriculture, transport, posts and telegraphs, labor, trade, commerce, finance, and education developed detailed programs for implementing the plan.

----

[7]Ibid., ix-x.

As he studied the Soviet planning process, Counts was impressed by the important role that had been given to education and to schools. He commented that the relationship of the Planning Commission to education was one of "the most striking features" of the Soviet state and might, indeed, determine the "fate of the revolutionary movement."[8]

Counts's comments on the importance that the Soviets gave to education in the planning process were made at the same time that he was criticizing American educators for being aloof from social, economic, and political involvement. In the Soviet Union, organized education was an instrument of national policy; in the United States it was not. Soviet educators were committed to stimulating a revolutionary consciousness and a planning attitude; American educators were content to be neutral and not take a stand on the great issues of the day. While Counts distrusted the antidemocratic and totalitarian tendencies inherent in the Soviet system, he believed that the Soviet leadership had recognized the power of education and was determined to use that power to advance its cause. It troubled him that American leaders had not recognized education's power as an instrument of modernization and change.

In 1931 Counts identified what he believed were the five controlling concepts of Soviet society: (1) Marxist-Leninist dialectical materialism; (2) a collectivism that emphasized proletarian sociopolitical unity and economic integration; (3) equality of the various nationalities of the Soviet Union; (4) equality of the sexes; (5) and industrialism. He saw these five concepts as providing the ideological context of Soviet society and as identifying national goals. Of the concepts he identified as controlling Soviet society, "industrialism" and "collectivism" were particularly relevant to Counts's analysis of American civilization. He astutely identified industrialism as the major force for change in the modern world. In Secondary Education and Industrialism, in 1929, Counts commented on the momentous impact of industrialism on society and education. He saw industrialism as the

---

[8]Ibid., 63-64.

major force in bringing about a technological society. His study of the Soviet Union convinced him that the Soviets were bent on modernizing their society by a comprehensive plan of industrialization. Writing during the Depression, Counts believed that the United States, already an industrial society, was entering a technological era. However, industrialism in the United States, under the aegis of economic individualism, was unplanned and chaotic. The Depression was the unfortunate result of an uncoordinated economy.

During the 1930s Counts insisted that the emergent technological age would be one of collectivism. He identified collectivism as a guiding concept of Soviet society. He also believed that American society, like all modern societies, would be organized collectively. It was possible for a particular society to choose the kind of collectivism that it wanted. While the Soviets had identified Marxist-Leninist dialectical materialism as the ideological context for the modernization of the Soviet Union, Americans were to use their democratic cultural heritage as the ideological base for the technological social order that was emerging in the United States.

In the early 1930s, particularly at the time of his writing *The Soviet Challenge to America*, Counts, like many visitors to the Soviet Union, displayed a somewhat naive view of events related to Stalin's consolidation of power. Counts's views may have been the impressionistic product of his travels in the Soviet Union rather than based upon the more detached and critical scholarship that characterized his later writing.

In 1931 Counts misread the personality and growing power of Stalin. He wrote, for example, that while there was a dictatorship in Russia, it was not a "personal dictatorship" of "any one man," but was a "dictatorship of the Communist party." He commented that the Soviet Communist party was

> an organism throbbing with life in every one of its thousands of separate cells. In these small constituent units, which live within the larger units of society, every important question of policy is thoroughly examined. Out of the disputes, discus-

sions, and deliberations of little groups of Communists scattered throughout the country, influenced of course by local conditions and by all the forces at work in the life of the people, there gradually emerges a mass opinion or judgment known as the Party Line. Although the direction which this line takes may be powerfully affected by such personalities as Lenin, Trotsky, Stalin and others, it is not fashioned by them. Hard, adamant, and inflexible at a given moment, it is a product of the collective mind and may alter its course at any time. To its mandates even Stalin must yield, if he would not be destroyed, as Lenin did before him. And the dictatorship of the Party would presumably survive the death of any individual.[9]

When Counts's comprehensive work, *The Challenge of Soviet Education*, appeared in 1957, both Counts's and American attitudes to the Soviet Union had changed. The temporary alliance between the German Nazis and the Soviets in the Molotov-Ribbentrop Pact of 1939 had dismayed many liberals. Counts had waged a vigorous struggle against American Communists for control of the American Federation of Teachers in the period from 1939 to 1941. Counts and his friends in the trade unions had left the American Labor party to organize the Liberal party in New York. Winston Churchill's phrase, "an iron curtain," had become parlance. A bipolar world had been created in which most of the world's nations were aligned into either Communist or anti-Communist blocs. As a direct result of this, the United States experienced a political phenomenon known as McCarthyism.

For the Counts of the 1950s, the Soviet experience was not as unique as he once thought it to be. He recognized greater continuities between tsarist autocracy and Soviet totalitarianism. Increasingly, he saw Soviet culture and education in bold ideological terms. The ideology that ruled the Soviet Union and its educational institutions was best expressed by the term "Bolshevism", which put Marx's doctrines into a form that was heavily influenced by the Russian past.

---

[9]Ibid., 42.

THE EDUCATOR AS SOCIAL THEORIST

By 1957 Counts identified four major foundational sources of Soviet education: (1) the doctrines of Karl Marx; (2) the practices of tsarist autocracy; (3) a body of liberal and humanistic ideas that had developed in the late nineteenth and early twentieth centuries; and (4) revolutionary absolutism or revolutionary Machiavellianism. While each of these four sources had an impact on Soviet education, Counts believed that the tradition of "revolutionary absolutism or revolutionary Machiavellianism" was the key to understanding Soviet education.[10] Developing in the mid-nineteenth century, revolutionary Machiavellianism stressed revolution by a tightly organized and disciplined minority of intellectuals committed to a utopian vision of the ideal society. It was Lenin's adherence to this concept that gave Bolshevism its particular character.

Revolutionary absolutism stemmed from the thought, writings, and activities of such men as Peter Zaichnevsky (1842-1896), Peter N. Tkachev (1844-1886), and Sergei Nechaiev (1847-1883). They called for the violent overthrow of the autocracy, the seizure of power by a militant minority, and the establishment of a ruthless dictatorship. These revolutionary absolutists called for an army in which the higher ranks, the vanguard, led the masses who were committed to unquestioned obedience. This army, whose membership was secret, was to follow conspiratorial modes of operation.

From the standpoint of educational foundations, Counts saw Tkachev as exerting a special influence on Lenin and on Bolshevism. Tkachev's conception of the principle of revolutionary "jumps" was central to Bolshevism. An anti-Marxist concept that was similar to Fascism's glorification of the will, Tkachev's theory of revolutionary "jumps" argued that not all societies were determined to pass through the same developmental stages. Because of special conditions, Russia might "jump" from feudalism to socialism without passing through capitalism. Since Russian tsarism was feeble and decadent, it could be overthrown by a resolute and disciplined minority. The theorists of revolutionary

---

[10]Counts, *The Challenge of Soviet Education*, 24.

absolutism rejected reform by gradualism, education, enlightenment, and liberal toleration. For example, Tkachev's appeal of 1862 called for a "bloody and merciless revolution" in which a "river of blood" would be shed and innocent victims would perish.[11]

Whereas in 1931 Counts had tended to see educational policy in the Soviet Union developed through extensive discussion and debate in the various cells, local organizations, and committees of the Communist party, his perception in the 1950s stressed the conspiratorial nature of a revolutionary Machiavellianism in Soviet policy formulation and implementation. According to Counts:

> In the thought of Tkachev, we may see the essential spirit of Soviet education—the employment of all educational institutions and processes for the building of an ideal society and the transformation of human nature under the ever watchful and ruthless direction of a "morally and intellectually developed" revolutionary minority—the Central Committee of the Communist party of the Soviet Union.[12]

As he wrote in 1957, Counts also commented that the Communist party of the Soviet Union was "not a political party . . . in the sense in which the term is employed in free societies." In its "organization and function," it is a "kind of political army designed to rule the Soviet Union, build a Communist order, and direct the course of a worldwide movement to overthrow the system of capitalism everywhere."[13]

For Counts, Soviet Communism had an international and messianic revolutionary vision. Lenin and his fellow Bolsheviks saw their revolution as a continuing one that was to spread triumphantly from Russia to all countries; in short, it would carry their system of society, ideology, and morals throughout the world. Counts warned:

---

[11]Ibid., 27.

[12]Ibid., 31.

[13]Ibid., 42.

Only the more gullible leaders of the free world will assume in the absence of deeds that the struggle will now and in the future take on the character of a peaceful and friendly competition. The fact should not be forgotten that the Central Committee, as it repudiates Stalin, places Lenin and all his works on a still higher pedestal. The "cult of personality survives."[14]

When one compares *The Soviet Challenge to America*, written in 1931, with *The Challenge of Soviet Education* in 1957, it is clear that Counts's attitudes toward the Soviet Union and its system of education had changed. In 1931 Counts wrote from a position that was not unsympathetic to the social and economic changes that were taking place in the Soviet Union. He was impressed by the way in which the Soviet population and state agencies had been mobilized to achieve the goals of the First Five Year Plan. He tended to see the Soviet people as responsive to the Communist leadership and also saw the Communist party as responsive to the popular will. In many respects, his affirmative response to Soviet social planning paralleled the ideas he expressed in his works on American education: to wit, the need for social planning and for an education that encouraged that goal.

At the time of his early studies of Soviet education, it is possible that Counts's scholarship lacked maturity. On his visits to the Soviet Union, he was influenced by the visible impressions of the industrial modernization of the Soviet Union. He emphasized that the Soviet Union would become a leading world power. He credited the Soviet leadership with transforming Russia from an industrially backward nation—with a high degree of illiteracy—into a literate and technologically advanced nation. Like many American liberals of the early 1930s, he was optimistic that the Soviet Union might become an example of a planning society that was coordinating its efforts to progress.

Some twenty-six years later in 1957, Counts was now making his analysis of Soviet education from a distance and had become more of a student of Russian history. He now recognized greater

---

[14]Ibid.

continuities in the Russian historical experience and saw more parallels between tsarist autocracy and Soviet dictatorship. His examination of Soviet education came to focus increasingly on the conspiratorial nature of Bolshevism as developed by Lenin and Stalin. The Communist party, Counts wrote, was following a general policy of Machiavellian absolutism. While it directed the entire course of events in the Soviet Union, it did so rigidly and with little popular involvement.

In some respects, Counts's views of the Soviet Union were those common to many American liberals and progressives. First, they saw the Soviet experiment as a sharp break with the reactionary Russian past, an experiment that in time might become humanitarian and popularly directed. Second, Counts and many other liberals became disenchanted with the emergence of Soviet totalitarianism and with the shifts in Soviet foreign policy that did violence to liberal aspirations. Third, Counts, a determined opponent of Soviet ideology, had become a Cold War warrior.

Chapter 10

George S. Counts and American Political Reform

Earlier chapters have examined George S. Counts's conception of American civilization. While the analysis has focused on
his response to the Depression of the 1930s, the social, political,
economic, and educational implications of Counts's theory transcended that crisis-torn decade. Although some of Counts's rhetoric must be viewed in the climate of the 1930s, his conception
of American civilization is significant as a qualitative cultural
theory of modernization, one that anticipated the more quantitative analyses that have appeared since the early 1960s.

The focus on Counts in the 1930s, which was featured in the
earlier chapters, needs to be considered in terms of the history
of educational ideas and as educational biography. The Depression decade had formative effects on Counts's professional life.
In the thirty-five years of his life that followed the Depression,
Counts's ideas continued to develop, mature, and change; however, there was an essential consistency in his ideas. He continued to see education as a comprehensive cultural force that
functioned within the context of American social, political, and
educational reform movements of the twentieth century. This
concluding chapter attempts to locate Counts as a social theorist
within the framework of American social and political thought.

Early Influences

To begin, it is important to consider the impact of Counts's
early environment as a contributing factor. Counts, a child of

the American middle border, spent his childhood and youth in rural Kansas at the turn of the century. Reared on a farm, he could still feel the impact of America's frontier experience. His family was Methodist in religious persuasion. The combination of rural cooperation at harvesting and threshing time as well as the community values associated with Methodism contributed to Counts's emphasis on the role of the group and the community in American life.[1]

In emphasizing group experience, community life, and mutuality of interests, Counts embraced the general orientation that pervaded the social and educational ideas of his colleagues in educational theory. John Dewey, reared in small-town Vermont, and William Heard Kilpatrick, a son of rural Georgia, stressed the importance of face-to-face and direct experience in the life of the American community, where human beings lived and learned in mutual association. They viewed the town-meeting approach to solving American political and social problems as an effective process in defining, discussing, and deliberating about and resolving community issues.

While Counts, Dewey, and Kilpatrick valued the social and educational significance of the shared human association that once existed in rural and small-town America, their perspective was not nostalgic. These progressive educational theorists took a reconstructive and experimental stance that underlined the process of change. Counts, especially, became impressed with the effects of the dynamics of modernization on American politics, economics, education, and society. He continually reemphasized the view that the great transformation wrought by the emergence of an industrial and technological order had profound ramifications for American culture.

Counts's reading of American history convinced him that freehold farm society and the frontier spirit of mutuality were an important legacy in the American experience. But in his view, this cooperative, sharing sense of community had to be recon-

---

[1]Gerald L. Gutek, "George Sylvester Counts (1889-1974): A Biographical Memoir," *Proceedings of the National Academy of Education* (Stanford: National Academy of Education, 1976) 333-53.

structed in bolder and more pervasive terms. For American democracy to work in a technological era, community association could no longer be construed in parochial or limited terms. The American nation had to be a national community—a Great Society—composed of sharing, planning, and coordinating citizens.

The Pragmatic Perspective

In the first half of the twentieth century, pragmatist philosophy, particularly Dewey's instrumentalism, dominated the theory of American educators. While remnants of philosophical idealism still existed, derived from William T. Harris's long-standing influence, the mainstream of American educational philosophy was clearly pragmatist. George S. Counts, in the Dewey-influenced philosophical mainstream, took a generally progressive and experimental posture toward social and educational issues. John Childs, his colleague at Columbia's Teachers College, wrote that Counts thought of "man and society in evolutionary and functional terms, of human behavior as essentially interactive and adaptive in nature, of learning as a function of this adaptive process, and of man as both a creature and a creator of culture."[2] In Childs's judgment, Counts subscribed fully to the pragmatist emphasis on evolutionary principles, experimental methods, and democratic values.

For pragmatists like Counts, change was the basic characteristic of human physical and social life. The American experience, shaped by changing agricultural and industrial frontiers, was highly receptive to the pragmatic orientation. As a youth in rural Kansas, Counts had seen people working to change the natural environment and adapt it to their needs. When the environment was altered, so were the patterns of human life. The westward-advancing frontiersman made contact with varying environments; and in adapting to the seacoasts, woodlands, prairies, and mountains, the American frontier experience was created. Since the day that Frederick Jackson Turner had presented

---

[2]John L. Childs, *American Pragmatism and Education* (New York: Henry Holt and Co., 1956) 214.

his thesis, the frontier had influenced the interpretations of American historians and social theorists. As the frontiersman struggled to master the wilderness, a condition of constant flux and changing social patterns characterized his interaction with the natural environment. Success in meeting the challenge of changing environments caused Americans to develop a social philosophy that was based on and encouraged change. As the agricultural frontier moved relentlessly westward, the older northern and eastern areas of the United States, too, experienced a new transformation caused by an expansive industrialism. Counts, the proponent of modernization, had a vision of the American heritage that derived from the frontier. He envisioned not the closing of the frontier, but rather its extension to new areas of American life and culture.

In contrast to the Social Darwinist defenders of a classical liberal status quo, Counts subscribed to the theories of such reform Darwinists as Lester F. Ward, George H. Mead, and John Dewey, who argued that human intelligence could be applied to the transformation of the environment. These advocates of social reform argued that change could be rationally and deliberately directed. By deliberate scientific planning, human beings could alter their environment according to their purposes and needs. Using the scientific method as an instrument to direct deliberate change, people could harness the forces of nature as they had once tamed the frontier wilderness. The pragmatic view of society, which encouraged the reforming impulse of progressivism in American politics, also served as a rationale for progressive educators who wanted to reform American education. The pragmatic view of life and society had stimulated the reconstruction of American law, sociology, politics, and education.

Counts's enthusiasm for planned social reform stemmed not only from the pragmatic persuasion in American thought but also from his commitment to the doctrine of progress. Although he did not have a deterministic view of the inevitability of progress, Counts did see human history as the record of humanity's ongoing achievements in mastering the forces of nature and gaining control over the environment. Early in his academic career Counts had begun but never completed a manuscript entitled *The Story of Human Progress*.[3] His antipathy to medievalism and his enthusiasm for progress made Counts a true descendant of the Enlightenment philosophers.

Counts's commitment to progress fitted nicely with his orientation toward philosophical pragmatism. Humankind, through experimental trial-and-error processes, had successfully conquered the natural environment. Human beings were not limited to mere environmental adjustment, however, but could use their funded knowledge and past experience to continue to transform both the natural and social environments. The modern industrial and technological environment, created by human minds and hands, could be transformed and reconstructed into a rationally planned, collectively controlled, and socially integrated society.

With the industrial revolution, the human environment had grown into a vast urban complex. As Counts viewed American society in the Depression-ridden 1930s, he concluded that this industrial society could remain a human jungle characterized by ruthless competition for survival or it could be transformed through cooperative planning and sharing into an efficient society of shared abundance. Counts's thesis, based on a faith in human rationality, argued that Americans could chart their destiny by deliberately directing social change. His projected "democratic collectivism" was a form of social engineering by which Americans could control the industrial and technological complex of modern society. Education was to be one of the instruments that would prepare Americans for the emergent society by raising their consciousness and by cultivating planning skills. Through the instruments of democracy and technology, Counts believed that Americans could control and harness their national environment for social welfare.

---

[3]George S. Counts, "The Story of Human Progress," unpublished MS in the Special Collections/Morris Library, Southern Illinois University of Carbondale.

The New History

Counts's theory of American civilization was a synthesis that integrated significant scholarship into an argument for planned social change. In particular, Counts relied heavily on the "new history" of Charles A. Beard and Carl Becker.[4] The essential pragmatic currents that were evident in the politics of the progressive era were reflected in the writings of the new progressive historians.[5] Like progressive politicians and educators, Becker and Beard—heirs to the pragmatic emphasis on the relevance of time and circumstance to truth and value—manifested confidence in the practical, technological, and experimental mode of solving modern social problems.[6]

Becker and Beard saw history as a continuing revision of the past based on the historian's values and tempered by his particular time, circumstances, and personality. History, so conceived, became the record of humankind's functional adjustment to the environment in order to satisfy needs arising in particular cultural situations.[7] It became a projection of the ideas and interests of the present upon past experience.[8] The new historians operated in the realm of value as well as fact, in that they recognized and used values to reinterpret past events. For them, history was an instrument to aid in solving contemporary problems. Challenging allegedly objective "scientific history," new historians such as Becker believed that human purposes, interests, and values were the proper areas of historical research.[9]

---

[4]Lloyd R. Sorenson, "Charles A. Beard and German Historical Thought," *Mississippi Valley Historical Review* 42 (September 1953): 275.

[5]Richard Hofstadter, *The Progressive Historians* (New York: Alfred A. Knopf, 1968).

[6]Cushing Strout, *The Pragmatic Revolt in American History: Carl Becker and Charles Beard* (New Haven: Yale University Press, 1958) 7.

[7]Ibid.

[8]Conyers Read, "The Social Responsibilities of the Historian," *American Historical Review* 55 (January 1950): 280.

[9]Carl L. Becker, *Progress and Power* (Stanford: Stanford University Press, 1958) 7.

Counts's views of American society and education closely paralleled Beard's economic interpretation of American history.[10] Beard frequently contributed to *The Social Frontier*, a journal edited by Counts. Counts used the relativism embodied in the new history to argue for cultural and educational relativism. Robert E. Mason, in *Educational Ideas in American Society*, observed that the new history profoundly affected educational theory by its stress on social problems. No longer conceived of as a purely objective discipline, history became a tool to guide human effort in reconstructing the contemporary social order.[11]

Counts, who acknowledged his indebtedness to Beard's *Economic Origins of Jeffersonian Democracy* and *The Economic Basis of Politics*, stressed economic interests as the basis of politics and the importance of freehold farmers as the originators of American democracy. Both Beard and Counts agreed that the wide distribution of land ownership on the frontier had engendered a state of economic equality that in turn produced political and social egalitarianism.[12]

Like Counts, Beard used the ideas of John Taylor to illustrate American egalitarianism in contrast to Hamiltonian special interests. Taylor, who claimed that a new class had emerged based on profits made from inflated paper money, bank stock, and the protective tariff, observed that the conflict between capitalistic and agrarian interests had led to the formation of American political parties.[13] Beard had used Taylor's arguments to examine the origin of American political parties on the basis of economic class. Counts had used Taylor's definition of a minority to define the term "economic aristocracy" and to describe the

---

[10]The long personal friendship of Beard and Counts is documented in the Counts/Beard Correspondence in Special Collections.

[11]Robert E. Mason, *Educational Ideas in American Society* (Boston: Allyn and Bacon Co., 1960) 81.

[12]Charles A. Beard, *The Economic Basis of Politics* (New York: Alfred A. Knopf, 1934) 67, 83.

[13]Charles A. Beard, *Economic Origins of Jeffersonian Democracy* (New York: MacMillan Co., 1927) 351-52.

ascendancy of this minority to dominance of social, economic, and political life in the United States.

During the 1930s Beard, like Counts, advocated social and economic planning. In *Toward Civilization*, 1930, Beard argued that residues of an inherited rural mentality were impeding the formulation of the ethical system needed in an engineering age. Contending that technical rationality rested on an economic base, Beard believed it possible to create a new civilization with ethical potentialities that had been inconceivable in a marginal economy. Within the scientific method, he concluded, lay the possibilities of both plan and control.[14] Counts extended Beard's argument for the permeation of engineering rationality into American life in *The Social Foundations of Education*. In *America in Midpassage*, 1939, Beard wrote:

> George S. Counts of the Teachers' College at Columbia University drew up in 1938 an impressive balance sheet of assets and liabilities in *The Prospects of American Democracy*, laid down a program of constructive action, and issued a call for a concert of popular powers in America.[15]

In constructing his social and educational theory, Counts relied on the new history as an interpretation of the American past that emphasized the cooperative and egalitarian life of the American freehold and frontier. Counts's interpretation of American civilization was not written for purely academic interests, but rather as an instrument to solve contemporary economic, social, political, and educational problems. As such, the new history was to be a guide to the past that directed present inquiry and shaped future activity.

Counts's social theory was derived from a particular interpretation of American history that emphasized Jeffersonianism, populism, and progressivism as vital elements in the heritage. He sought to relate these elements to modern American society.

---

[14]Charles A. Beard, *Toward Civilization* (New York: Longmans, Green & Co., 1930) 301-303.

[15]Charles Beard and Mary Beard, *Americans in Midpassage* (New York: MacMillan Co., 1939) 921-22.

Counts saw Jeffersonian social egalitarianism, with its origins on the agrarian frontier, as the foundation of American democracy. The Jeffersonian tradition had been challenged by the ascendancy of the capitalistic, laissez-faire, individualistic economic tradition that Counts called Hamiltonianism. The new American society could follow either Jeffersonian democracy or Hamiltonian aristocracy. Counts argued for a revitalized Jeffersonianism as a means of creating a popular, equalitarian, democratic American society.

Counts used the new history, especially Beard's version, to create a frame of reference for his theory of cultural reconstruction. His use of the new history was ideological in that it furnished a historical rationale for his projected new social order. The frame of reference that the new history provided was a selective perspective of America's past that was to be put to work as an ideological instrument to create a particular vision of America's future.

Political Position

George Counts was a political man as well as a scholar. Like the Athenian in ancient Greece's age of democracy, Counts believed that a truly functioning man was an informed participant in the politics of his polis. Although he remained in the framework of modern American political progressivism and liberalism, Counts preferred a position on the political continuum that was often decidedly left-of-center. Of his politics, he wrote:

> I regard myself as a cross between a Jeffersonian Democrat and a Lincolnian Republican, struggling with the old problem of human freedom and equality in the age of science and technology. I enjoy surprising my students by telling them that I am a conservative, that I have striven throughout my life to "conserve our radical tradition."[16]

---

[16]George S. Counts, "A Humble Autobiography," in Robert J. Havighurst, ed., *Leaders of American Education: The Seventieth Yearbook of the National Society for the Study of Education* (Chicago: University of Chicago Press, 1971) 164.

Counts's voting record in American presidential elections revealed his preference for progressive and liberal candidates over those of a more conservative persuasion. In 1912 he voted for Theodore Roosevelt, candidate of the Progressive party; in 1916 for Woodrow Wilson, the Democratic standard-bearer; in 1920 for James Cox, a Democrat; in 1924 he again supported a third-party candidate, Robert LaFollette, a Progressive; in 1928 his choice was the Democrat, Alfred E. Smith; in 1932, in the Depression's darkest hours, he voted for Norman Thomas, the Socialist party nominee. In the elections of 1936, 1940, and 1944, he endorsed Franklin D. Roosevelt, the Democrat, whose New Deal he generally supported; in 1948 Harry Truman was his choice. In 1952 and 1956 he voted for Adlai Stevenson, the Democrat; in 1960 for John F. Kennedy; in 1964 for Lyndon B. Johnson; and in 1968 for Hubert H. Humphrey—all nominees of the Democratic party.

An analysis of his voting behavior in presidential elections tells something about Counts's orientation in national politics. Consistently, he voted for candidates who promised to reform, renew, or reconstruct American life. Clearly, he favored candidates who were political progressives. He supported those who have been identified as the leading progressives of their day: Theodore Roosevelt, Woodrow Wilson, and Robert LaFollette.

Although Counts saw the American cultural heritage as a unique experience, he was not an isolationist. At times, his close friend, Charles A. Beard, veered in the isolationist direction, but Counts maintained an international perspective. His travels to Asia and his intense study of Soviet culture and education broadened his outlook. Most likely, Counts favored President Wilson's efforts to create a world order governed by international law. Counts's vote for James Cox in 1920 indicated his support for American involvement in world affairs and a rejection of Warren Harding's promise to return to "normalcy."

In 1928 Counts voted for Governor Alfred E. Smith, the first Roman Catholic to be nominated for the presidency by a major political party. Counts did not support the great engineer and planner, Herbert Hoover, the Republican candidate in 1928 and 1932, largely because Hoover's articulate endorsement of individualism was exactly what Counts opposed when he made appeals for a collective democracy.

Counts's vote for Norman Thomas in the election of 1932 is of special interest. Like many intellectuals, Counts found the early years of the Great Depression to be particularly distressing. In the election of 1932, Hoover's administration was discredited by its unwillingness to use the federal government to meet the challenges raised by the breakdown of the economic system and massive unemployment. While Franklin Roosevelt was an alternative, his campaign seemed to rely more on personal dynamism rather than bold policies of reform. Discontented with both major parties, many intellectuals turned to the Socialist candidate, Norman Thomas.

When Roosevelt's New Deal program was revealed in the emergency legislation of "the Hundred Days" and in such measures as the Civilian Conservation Corps, the National Industrial Recovery Act, and the Works Progress Administration, Counts came to support these policies intended to speed recovery and stimulate reform. His voting record shows support of Roosevelt's campaigns for a second, third, and fourth term. Counts, who was acutely critical of the efforts of the Liberty League to defeat Roosevelt, believed the league represented the economic aristocracy that he attacked in his *Prospects of American Democracy.* While he agreed with the basic direction of Roosevelt's New Deal, he criticized it as a piecemeal attempt at reform rather than a comprehensive national reconstruction of the American social, political, and economic system.

Although he had supported third-party candidates in 1912, 1924, and 1932, Counts did not support Henry Wallace's bid on the Progressive party ticket in 1948. Instead, he voted for Harry Truman, the Democratic incumbent. Counts's voting record in presidential elections serves as a context to examine his own direct political activity. In New York State, Counts was active in the American Labor party, which was organized in 1936. In 1941 he was an unsuccessful candidate of the American Labor party for the New York City Council.

A year later, in 1942, Counts was elected chairman of the American Labor party, which had endorsed a platform that stressed: (1) support for the war effort; (2) support for organized labor; (3) an excess profit tax on industries involved in war production; (4) consumer protection; (5) rent ceilings; (6) municipal construction of power plants; (7) extension of social security benefits; (8) educational programs for the unemployed; (9) state health insurance; (10) increased protection for women workers; (11) preservation of civil liberties; (12) increased inheritance and corporation taxes; (13) farmer cooperatives; and (14) efforts to achieve postwar planning.[17] In many respects, the American Labor platform resembled a scaled-down version of the program of action that Counts had recommended in his *Prospects of American Democracy.*

Like many left-of-center, third-party efforts, the American Labor party was beset by contending factions. Counts was a leader of the more conservative, anti-Communist wing of the party. When the left wing came to dominate the party, Counts and his associates left to form the Liberal party.

In the election of 1952, Counts was the Liberal candidate for the United States Senate. An examination of the issues raised by Counts in his campaign reveals his position as a political activist. In accepting his party's nomination, Counts advocated:

1. "Achieving a just and durable peace" that "could be won by marshalling all the forces of the free world to turn back imperialistic Soviet ambitions."
2. Creating a "stable economy" to bring "opportunity, security and well-being to all."
3. "The strengthening of the tradition of political liberty and cultural freedom under the rule of law."
4. "The extension of the benefits of democracy to all people, particularly the Negroes."
5. "Establishment of a high level of efficiency and honesty in government at all levels."

---

[17]*New York Times,* 23 August 1942.

6. "The raising of living standards in America" to achieve "a rich and good life for the individual without regard to race, creed, or national origin."[18]

During his senatorial campaign, Counts attacked Mc-Carthyism as being "both superficial and ineffectual" and "destructive of the civil liberties we cherish in our country." While opposed to McCarthyism, Counts called for a thorough study of Communism so that people would understand its totalitarian nature. He also urged that "we must be sure that the Communist party does not penetrate the teaching profession and our educational system."[19] When the votes were counted, Counts had received 461,229, the largest vote polled by a Liberal candidate since the party's founding in 1944. The victor was Irving Ives, the Republican, who polled 3,811,255, followed by John Cashmore, the Democrat, with 2,533,373. Corliss Lamont, the American-Labor-party candidate, received 98,839.[20]

As a leader in the Liberal party, Counts and his associates were in a political position that resembled that of the Fabians in the British Labour party. The Liberals hoped to move New York's Democratic party to a left-of-center position and even perhaps to influence national politics.

In a broad sense, political and educational theory are intimately related. Plato's *Republic*, for instance, was an educational as well as a political treatise. Rousseau's *Emile* was the educational companion to his social-contract theory. In similar fashion, Counts's educational theory had political implications. As a political activist, he presented an educational point of view to his listeners.

Counts's left-of-center politics were rooted in American political protest and reform movements such as Populism, Progressivism, and Liberalism. Although aware of European ideological movements, Counts believed that American politics,

[18]Ibid., 9 September 1952.
[19]Ibid., 5 October 1952.
[20]Ibid., 6 November 1952.

like American education, grew out of the cultural heritage that was uniquely American.

George S. Counts was a contributor to social and educational theory. At times, he was a scholarly commentator on matters that were pedagogical or school-oriented. At other times, he was a polemicist for a new social order. At still other times, he was a political activist, union leader, and organizer. The contribution of such a man is difficult to summarize, since each of these roles deserves its own assessment. If there is any phrase that captures his contribution to American life, it is perhaps that he was an ideologist on behalf of a democratic conception and program of education for the United States. He was an ideologist in the sense that he had developed an interpretation of the American past oriented toward a future program of action that embraced politics, society, and education.

Bibliography

Manuscripts and Letters

The George S. Counts Papers, Special Collections/Morris Library, Southern Illinois University at Carbondale.

Copies of the following items were given to the author by George S. Counts in December 1961:

Counts, George S. Letter to Dean William F. Russell of Teachers College, Columbia University, 19 January 1931.

_____. "The Meaning of a Liberal Education in Industrial Society." N.d.

_____. "A Proposal for Historical and Cultural Foundations at Columbia." N.d.

_____. "A Proposal for the Establishment at Teachers College of an Institute for the Study of the Historical and Cultural Foundations of American Education." N.d.

_____. "Proposed Study of Education and Culture in an American Industrial Community." N.d.

_____. "Some Thoughts on the Organization of an Institute of Social Research at Teachers College." N.d.

_____. "Tentative Plan for the Organization of an Institute of Social Research at Teachers College." N.d.

Books

Bailyn, Bernard. *Education in the Forming of American Society.* New York: W. W. Norton and Co., 1972.

Beard, Charles A. *The Economic Basis of Politics.* New York: Alfred A. Knopf, 1934.

——————. *The Economic Origins of Jeffersonian Democracy.* New York: The MacMillan Co., 1927.

——————. *Toward Civilization.* New York: Longmans, Green, and Co., 1930.

Beard, Charles and Mary Beard. *America in Midpassage.* New York: The MacMillan Co., 1939.

Becker, Carl L. *Progress and Power.* Stanford: Stanford University Press, 1935.

Bellamy, Edward. *Looking Backward.* New York: The New American Library, 1960.

Berle, A. A. and G. C. Means. *The Modern Corporation and Private Property.* New York: Commerce Clearing House, 1932.

Black, C. E. *The Dynamics of Modernization: A Study in Comparative History.* New York: Harper and Row Publishers, 1966.

Bowers, C. A. *The Progressive Educator and the Depression: The Radical Years.* New York: Random House, 1969.

Casson, Stanley. *Progress and Catastrophe.* New York: Harper and Brothers Publishers, 1937.

Chase, Stuart. *A New Deal.* New York: The MacMillan Co., 1932.

Childs, John L. *American Pragmatism and Education.* New York: Henry Holt and Co., 1956.

Childs, John L. and George S. Counts. *America, Russia, and the Communist Party in the Postwar World.* New York: The John Day Co., 1943.

Committee of the Progressive Education Association on Social and Economic Problems. *A Call to the Teachers of the Nation.* New York: The John Day Co., 1933.

Counts, George S. *The American Road to Culture: A Social Interpretation of Education in the United States.* New York: The John Day Co., 1930.

——————. *The Challenge of Soviet Education.* New York: McGraw-Hill, 1957.

Counts, George S. and Nucia P. Lodge. *The Country of the Blind: The Soviet System of Mind Control.* Boston: Houghton-Mifflin Co., 1948.

Counts, George S. *Dare the School Build a New Social Order?* New York: The John Day Co., 1932.

_____. *Educacao para uma sociedade de homens livres na era tecnologica*. Rio de Janeiro: Centro Brasileiro de Pesquisas educacionais, 1958.

_____. *Education and American Civilization*. New York: Teachers College, Columbia University, Bureau of Publications, 1952.

_____. *Education and the Foundations of Human Freedom*. Pittsburgh: University of Pittsburgh Press, 1962.

_____. *Education and the Promise of America*. New York: The MacMillan Co., 1946.

_____. *The Education of Free Men in American Democracy*. Washington: National Education Association, 1941.

_____. *A Ford Crosses Soviet Russia*. Boston: Stratford Co., 1930.

Counts, George S. and J. C. Chapman. *Principles of Education*. Boston: Houghton-Mifflin Co., 1924.

Counts, George S. *The Prospects of American Democracy*. New York: The John Day Co., 1938.

_____. *School and Society in Chicago*. New York: Harcourt, Brace, and Co., 1928.

_____. *The Schools Can Teach Democracy*. New York: The John Day Co., 1939.

_____. *Secondary Education and Industrialism*. Cambridge: Harvard University Press, 1929.

_____. *The Selective Character of American Secondary Education*. Chicago: University of Chicago Press, 1922.

_____. *The Senior High School Curriculum*. Chicago: University of Chicago Press, 1926.

_____. *The Social Composition of Boards of Education*. Chicago: University of Chicago Press, 1927.

_____. *The Social Foundations of Education*. New York: Charles Scribner's Sons, 1934.

_____. *The Soviet Challenge to America*. New York: The John Day Co., 1931.

Cremin, Lawrence A. *Public Education*. New York: Basic Books, Inc., 1976.

_____. *The Transformation of the School*. New York: Alfred A. Knopf, 1961.

Curti, Merle. *The Social Ideas of American Educators*. Patterson NJ: Littlefield, Adams, and Co., 1959.

Dennis, Lawrence J. and William E. Eaton. *George S. Counts: Educator for a New Age*. Carbondale: Southern Illinois Press, 1980.

Dewey, John. *Democracy and Education*. New York: MacMillan Co., 1916.

——————. *Individualism, Old and New*. New York: Minton, Balch, and Co., 1930.

——————. *Liberalism and Social Action*. New York: P. G. Putnam's Sons, 1935.

Educational Policies Commission. *The Unique Function of Education in American Democracy*. Washington: National Education Association, 1937.

Gutek, Gerald L. *The Educational Theory of George S. Counts*. Columbus: Ohio State University Press, 1970.

Havighurst, Robert J., ed. *Leaders in American Education: The Seventieth Yearbook of the National Society for the Study of Education, Part 2*. Chicago: University of Chicago Press, 1971.

Hofstadter, Richard. *The Progressive Historians: Turner, Beard, Parrington*. New York: Alfred A. Knopf, 1968.

——————. *Social Darwinism in American Thought*. Boston: Beacon Press, 1955.

Hoover, Herbert. *Addresses upon the American Road, 1933-1938*. New York: Charles Scribner's Sons, 1938.

——————. *The Memoirs of Herbert Hoover: The Great Depression, 1929-1941*. New York: The MacMillan Co., 1952.

Kavinoky, Edward H. and Julian Park, eds. *My Friends: Twenty-eight History Making Speeches by Franklin Delano Roosevelt*. Buffalo: Foster and Stewart Publishing Co., 1945.

Knight, Edgar W. *Education in the United States*. New York: Ginn and Co., 1934.

Mason, Robert E. *Educational Ideas in American Society*. Boston: Allyn and Bacon Co., 1960.

Padover, Saul K. *The Genius of America*. New York: McGraw-Hill Book Co., 1960.

President's Research Committee on Social Trends. *Recent Social Trends in the United States*. New York: McGraw-Hill Co., 1933.

Rauch, Basil. *The History of the New Deal, 1933-1938.* New York: Creative Age Press, Inc., 1944.

Strout, Cushing. *The Pragmatic Revolt in American History: Carl Becker and Charles Beard.* New Haven: Yale University Press, 1958.

Zevin, B. D., ed. *Nothing to Fear: The Selected Addresses of Franklin Delano Roosevelt.* Cambridge: The Riverside Press, 1946.

Articles

"The Association Faces its Opportunities." *Progressive Education* (9 May 1932): 229-31.

Callahan, Raymond S. "George S. Counts: Educational Statesman." In *Leaders in American Education: The Seventieth Yearbook of the National Society for the Study of Education.*

Carlson, Avis D. "Deflating the Schools." *Harper's Monthly Magazine* 167 (November 1933): 705-13.

Counts, George S. "Business and Education." *Teachers College Record* 39 (April 1938): 553-60.

——————. "Collectivism and Collectivism." *The Social Frontier* 1 (November 1934): 3-4.

——————. "Dare Progressive Education Be Progressive?." *Progressive Education* 9 (April 1932): 257-63.

——————. "Education and the Five Year Plan of Soviet Russia." *National Education Association Proceedings* 68 (1930): 213-18.

——————. "Education—For What? The Ten Fallacies of the Educators." *The New Republic* 71 (18 May 1932): 12-16.

——————. "A Humble Autobiography." In *Leaders in American Education: The Seventieth Yearbook of the National Society for the Study of Education.*

——————. "A Liberal Looks at Life." *Frontiers of Democracy* 7 (15 May 1941): 231-32.

——————. "The Place of the School in the Social Order." *National Education Association Proceedings* 64 (1926): 308-15.

——————. "Presentday Reasons for Requiring a Longer Period of Pre-Service Preparation for Teachers." *National Education Association Proceedings* 73 (1935): 694-701.

_____. "Secondary Education and the Social Problem." *School Executives Magazine* 51 (August 1932): 499-501, 519-20.

_____. "Theses on Freedom, Culture, Social Planning and Leadership." *National Education Association Proceedings* 70 (1932): 249-52.

_____. "To Vitalize American Tradition." *Progressive Education* 15 (March 1938): 245.

"Economics and the Good Life." *The Social Frontier* 2 (December 1935): 72-73.

"Educating for Tomorrow." *The Social Frontier* 1 (October 1934): 5-7.

"Freedom in a Collectivistic Society." *The Social Frontier* 1 (April 1935): 9-10.

Gutek, Gerald L. "George Sylvester Counts (1889-1974): A Biographical Memoir." *Proceedings of the National Academy of Education* 3 (1976): 333-53.

"Orientation." *The Social Frontier* 1 (October 1934): 3-5.

"The Position of the Social Frontier." *The Social Frontier* 1 (January 1935): 30-33.

Read, Conyers. "The Social Responsibilities of the Historian." *American Historical Review* 55 (January 1950): 275-85.

Sorenson, Lloyd R. "Charles A. Beard and German Historical Thought." *Mississippi Valley Historical Review* 42 (September 1953): 275-85.

"Teachers and the Class Struggle." *The Social Frontier* 2 (November 1935): 39-40.

Other Sources

Interview with George S. Counts by the author in Carbondale, Illinois, 21 December 1961.

New York Times, 23 August 1942; 9 September 1952; 5 October 1952; 6 November 1952.

Index

Adler, Mortimer, 124
America in Midpassage (Beard and Beard), 156
America, Russia, and the Communist Party in the Postwar World (Counts and Childs), 139
American Bankers Association, 87
American Civil Liberties Union, 116
American democratic heritage, 38-41, 61-70, 98-108
   roots of, 61-64
American Federation of Teachers, 85
   opposed Communist influence in, 10, 144
   president of, 10, 113
American Historical Association, 9
American Labor Party
   chairman of, 10, 144, 159-60
American Liberty League, 81, 87, 159
American Road to Culture, The (Counts, 12, 27, 133-34
"Arithmetic Tests and Studies in the Psychology of Arithmetic" (Counts), 10

Bailyn, Bernard, 133
Baker University, 5-6
Barnard, Henry, 17, 20
Beard, Charles A., 7, 13, 15, 17, 33-34, 85, 97, 101, 118, 131, 154-56, 158
Becker, Carl L., 154
Bellamy, Edward, 33
Berle, Adolph A., 90
Black, C. E., 47
Bobbitt, Franklin, 6-7
Bolsheviks, 137, 146
Bolshevism, 144, 145, 148
Butler, Nicholas Murray, 19-20

Callahan, Raymond E., 4-5
Cashmore, John, 161
Casson, Stanley, 55
Challenge of Soviet Education, The (Counts), 9, 139, 144, 147
Childs, John L., 7, 151
Churchill, Winston, 144
Civilian Conservation Corps, 159
Civilization Education
   and American social policy, 129-36
   Counts's Program of Action for, 111-22
   philosophy of, 29-33, 123-36
   relativistic, 124

resembled Dewey's instrumentalism, 123
school's position in society, 125-27
theoretical reconstruction in education, 127-29
Clayton Antitrust Acts, 73
Cold War of the 1950s, 31-32, 103, 148
Collectivism, 21-25, 143
democratic, 85, 98
economic, 82-84
origins of, 84-87
Commission of the American Historical Association on the Social Studies in the Schools, 7, 9, 12-13, 17, 34, 85
Commission on Recent Social Trends, 85
Communism, 40, 101-102, 119, 143-44, 146, 147-48
American, 10, 144
in American Federation of Teachers, 10
Country of the Blind: the Soviet System of Mind Control (Counts and Lodge), 9, 139
Counts, George Sylvester
in American Federation of Teachers, 123
analysis of democratic ethic, 38-41, 61-64, 67, 78, 98-108
analysis of economic individualism vs. collectivism, 21-25, 77-96
analysis of industrial civilization, 70-76
birth, 5
broadens definition of democracy, 64-66
characteristics of technology, 70-76
childhood, 5, 149-51
civilizational philosophy of education, 29-33, 108, 123-36

cultural lag theory, 51-55
death, 3, 14
decline of economic democracy, 64-66
education, 5-7
educational statesman, 4-10
emphasis on role of community, 150
foreign policy proposal, 120
frame of reference, 29-41
graduate student, 6-7
ideologist, 97-122
influenced by Charles A. Beard, 34, 154-57
leadership roles in technological economy, 110-11
marriage, 6
modernization theory, 43-48
on national educational commissions, 9
opposed formation of economic aristocracy, 89-96
origins of economic individualism, 77-79
political position, 157-62
politician, 10, 160-61
pragmatism's influence on, 151-53
in Progressive Educational Association, 123
reaction to Great Depression, 3-4, 15-28, 52-56
rise of industrial civilization, 36-38, 43
scholar and writer, 8, 10-14, 17
scientific movement in education, 10-12, 17, 70-72, 97-98
social theory, 3-4, 149-62
studies Soviet education and culture, 8-9, 31, 40, 84, 123, 137-48
supported teacher unionization, 10, 113
teacher, 6, 7-8
at Teachers College, Colum-

bia, 7, 123
urges social planning in edu-
    cation, 24-28, 108
Counts, James, father, 5
Counts, Lois Hazel Bailey, wife, 6
Counts, Mertie Gamble, mother, 5
Cox, James, 158
Craven, Avery O., 17, 85
Cremin, Lawrence, 133
Curti, Merle, 13, 20
"Dare Progressive Education Be
    Progressive?" (Counts), 12, 25-
    26, 140
Dare the School Build a New So-
    cial Order? (Counts), 4, 12, 21,
    26, 30, 32, 59, 66, 97, 108, 124,
    140
Debs, Eugene V., 33
Delaware College, 7
Democracy, 26, 131
    and collectivism, 98
    Counts broadens his definition
        of, 68-70
    Counts's educational philoso-
        phy for, 123-36
    decline of economic, 64-68
    economic foundations of, 62-
        63, 64-68
    effects of economics on, 34
    political foundations of, 65
    roots of, 61-64
    social foundations of, 65
Democracy and Education
    (Dewey), 77
Democratic ethic, 38-41, 64-66,
    67, 68, 131-32, 134
Depression of the 1930s, 3, 4, 12,
    13, 14, 29-30, 33, 43, 44, 51-52,
    64, 75, 77, 83, 97, 103
    Counts's response to, 3-4, 15-
        28, 52, 56
    effects on education, 17-20
de Tocqueville, Alexis, 63
Dewey, John, 7, 13, 15, 38, 48, 64,
    71, 77, 96, 101, 105, 123, 126,

131, 150, 152
    Complete Act of Thought, 71
    instrumentalism, 101, 123,
        151
Economic Basis of Politics, The
    (Beard), 155
Economic Origins of Jeffersonian
    Democracy (Beard), 155
Educacao para uma sociedade ho-
    mens liveres na era tecnologica
    (Counts), 59
Education
    and American social policy,
        129-36
    civilizational philosophy of,
        29-33, 123-36
    democratic ethic in, 38-41
    Depression's effect on, 17-20
    Program of Action for civic,
        111-22
    school's role in society, 125-27
    Soviet, 8, 117, 137-48, 158
    theoretical reconstruction in,
        127-29
Education and American Civili-
    zation (Counts), 14, 33, 36, 59,
    68, 69, 75, 95
Education and Industrialism
    (Counts), 37
Education and the Foundations of
    Human Freedom (Counts), 41,
    116
Education and the Promise of
    America (Counts), 32-33, 59,
    68
Education of Free Men in Ameri-
    can Democracy, The (Counts),
    13-14
Educational Ideas in American
    Society (Mason), 155
Educational Policies Commission
    of the National Educational
    Association, 9
Educational Survey Commission
    to the Philippines, 8

Emerson, Ralph Waldo, 64
Emile (Rousseau), 161
Enright, Homer K., 6
Fabians, 85, 161
Fascism, 16, 19, 38, 39, 40, 101-102, 119, 145
Ford, Henry, 52
Ford Crosses Soviet Russia, A (Counts), 8, 138-39
Fourteenth Amendment, U.S. Constitution, 91
Garibaldi, Giuseppe, 16
George, Henry, 33, 64
Goebbels, Joseph, 39
Grange, The, 84
Hamiltonian aristocracy, 157
Harding, Warren, 158
Harris, William Torrey, 17, 19-20
Harris Teachers College, 7
Hart, Joseph K., 6
Hitler, Adolf, 16, 30, 39, 71
    Third Reich, 30, 39
Homestead Act of 1862, 80
Hoover, Herbert C., 22-25, 27, 85, 103, 158, 159
    economic individualism, 22-23, 25
Humphrey, Hubert H., 158
Hutchins, Robert, 124
Ideologist
    definition, 98
Individualism, 21-25, 50-51
    Counts's analysis of, 87
    economic, 81-82
    origins of economic, 77-79
    types:
    capitalistic entrepreneur, 79-81, 89-94
    freehold farmer, 79-81
Individualism: Old and New (Dewey), 77
Industrialism
    effects on American civilization, 11-12, 16, 36-37, 43-48, 57, 70-76

Inquiry into the Principle and Policy of the Government of the United States (Taylor), 90
Ives, Irving, 161
I Want to Be Like Stalin (Counts and Lodge), 139
Jackson, Andrew, 64, 131
Jefferson, Thomas, 64, 92, 131
Jeffersonian democracy, 156-57
Johnson, F. Ernest, 7
Johnson, Lyndon B., 32, 49, 158
    Great Society, 32
    War on Poverty, 32, 49
Judd, Charles Hubbard, 6, 10
Kennedy, John F., 158
Kilpatrick, William Heard, 7, 13, 77, 150
Knight, Edgar W., 19
Know-Nothings, 107
Krey, A. C., 85
LaFollette, Robert, 158
Lamont, Corliss, 161
Landon, Alfred, 103
Leaders in American Education (Havighurst), 4
Lenin, N., 137, 144, 145, 146, 147, 148
Liberal party of New York, 85
    helped found, 10, 144
    nominated for U. S. Senate, 10
Liberalism, 161
Liberalism and Social Action (Dewey), 77
Lincoln, Abraham, 64
Lippmann, Walter, 4-5
Locke, John, 80
Lodge, Nucia P., 9
McAndrews, William, 11
MacArthur, Douglas, 9
McCarthy, Senator Joseph, 10
McCarthyism, 103, 144, 161
Malthus, Thomas, 33
Manchester School of Classical Economic Thought, 74

Mann, Horace, 17, 20, 64
Markham, O. G., 6
Marx, Karl, 144, 145
    dialectical materialism, 34, 71
    economic theories, 33
Mason, Robert E., 155
Mazzini, 16
Mead, George H., 152
Means, Gardiner C., 90
Merriam, Charles E., 7, 17, 85
Michigan State University, 8
The Modern Corporation and Private Property (Berle and Means), 90
Molotov-Ribbentrop Pact of 1939, 144
Moulton, Harold G., 7
Mussolini, Benito, 16, 30

National Education Association, 9
National Industrial Recovery Act, 159
Nazism, 38, 39, 71, 101-103
Nechaiev, Sergei, 145
New Deal, 4, 22, 23, 24, 25, 49, 81, 91, 101, 103, 107, 131, 158, 159
Newlon, Jesse, 7, 17, 85
Northwestern University, 8
Nye Committee, U. S. Senate, 119

Parmenter, Charles S., 6
Piotrak, M. M., 138
Plato, 161
Populism, 84, 161
Porter, Alice D., 6
Pre-Emption Act of 1841, 80
Principles of Education, The (Crosby and Counts), 125, 127
Progress and Catastrophe (Casson), 55
Progressive education, 25-26
Progressive Education Association, 9, 25, 83, 94
Progressivism, 84, 135-36, 161
Prospects of American Democracy, The (Counts), 13, 14, 23, 32, 38, 55, 68, 81, 90, 95, 97, 98,
    102, 118, 120, 140, 156, 159, 160
Puritans, 49

Republic (Plato), 161
Ricardo, David, 33
Roosevelt, Franklin D., 4, 22-25, 27, 49, 81, 92, 101, 103, 107, 114, 131, 158, 159
    New Deal, 4, 22, 23, 24, 25, 49, 81, 91, 101, 103, 107, 131, 158, 159
    Second Inaugural Address, 23-24
Roosevelt, Theodore, 158
Rosenberg, Alfred, 39
Rousseau, Jean J., 161
Rugg, Harold, 7
Russell, William F., 7
Russia, 31, 71
Russian education
    (see Soviet Education)

School and Society in Chicago (Counts), 11
Schools
    position in society, 125-27
Schools Can Teach Democracy, The (Counts), 13-14
Second Treatise on Government (Locke), 80
Secondary Education and Industrialism (Counts), 11-12, 142-43
Selective Character of American Secondary Education, The (Counts), 10-11, 31
Senior High School Curriculum, The (Counts), 31
Sherman Antitrust Acts, 73
Small, Albion W., 7, 10
Smith, Adam, 33
Smith, Alfred E., 81, 158
Social Composition of Boards of Education (Counts), 11
Social Darwinism, 50, 152

Social Foundations of Education, The (Counts), 12-13, 17-18, 72, 75, 85, 97, 118, 119, 130, 140, 156

Social Frontier, The, 13, 26, 36, 83, 86, 87, 89, 94, 95, 155

Southern Illinois University, 8

Soviet Challenge to America, The (Counts), 8, 139, 140, 143, 147

Soviet education, 8-9, 117, 142, 146-47, 158

    Department of Social Education, 138

    foundations of, 145-46

    impact on Counts's theory of American civilization, 137-48

Soviet Union

    controlling concepts of society, 142

    Counts's changing attitude toward, 139-40

    Counts's perspectives on Communism, 40, 143, 146

    Counts's travels in, 8-9, 31, 40, 137

    First Five-Year Plan, 8, 40, 138, 141, 147

    Five-Year Plans, 31, 38

    State Planning Commission, 141-42

Spencer, Herbert, 50, 55

Stalin, Josef, 16, 38, 143, 144, 147, 148

Starr, Frederick, 7

Stevenson, Adlai, 158

"Story of Human Progress, The" (Counts), 153

Sumner, William Graham, 50

Sumner County High School, 6

Supreme Court, U.S., 91, 114

Taylor, John, 90, 155-56

Teachers College, Columbia, 151

    associate director of International Institute, 8, 137

    faculty member at, 1927-1955, 7

Technology

    characteristics of, 72-76

    and democracy creates democratic collectivism, 98

    effects on civilization, 70-76

Thomas, Norman, 158-59

Thompson, William Hale, 11

Tkachev, Peter N., 145-46

Toward Civilization (Beard), 156

Trotsky, 144

Truman, Harry, 158, 159

Turner, Frederick Jackson, 151-52

Unionization, 113

U.S. Chamber of Commerce, 87

University of Chicago

    graduate study at, 6-7

    faculty, 7

University of Colorado, 7-8

University of Pittsburgh, 7

University of Washington, 7

Wallace, Henry, 159

Ward, Lester F., 152

Weimar Republic, Germany, 16

Whitman, Walt, 64

Wilson, Woodrow, 16, 131, 158

Works Progress Administration, 159

World War I, 15-16, 20-21, 44, 103, 119

World War II, 31-32, 44

Yale University, 7

Zaichnevsky, Peter, 145